The Inspiring Gardening Book for Kids

Ages 8-12

36 Flower Ideas to Create a Stunning Butterfly Garden: An Exploring Nature Activity Book

By Georges Fine

The Inspiring Gardening Book for Kids Ages 8-12
© Georges Fine, 2024
All rights reserved.

First edition, 2024
Independently Published

ISBN: 9798302477767
Printed by Amazon's Print-on-Demand Service at facilities worldwide.
Cover and Interior Design by: Georges FINE, with Canva, Affinity Publisher, ChatGPT.

Disclaimer: This book is designed for educational and recreational purposes only. The author assumes no responsibility for injuries, damages, or losses resulting from the use of the activities or gardening advice in this book. Children should always be supervised during gardening and craft activities. Consult an expert when handling toxic plants or insects.

Acknowledgments: A heartfelt thank-you to my family, friends, and early readers who supported this project.

For updates, resources, and more, visit: www.horizonlecture.com

Table of Content

Introduction

Plant the Seeds of Wonder and Growth

What if you could grow a garden bursting with color and buzzing with life—while discovering nature's secrets and becoming more curious, confident, and creative?

Gardening is more than planting seeds. It's an invitation to **explore nature's wonders, care for living things, and develop a positive mindset.** Imagine the joy of watching your flowers bloom after a little patience and care. Picture the excitement of seeing a caterpillar transform into a butterfly or harvesting seeds to plant again next year. Gardening teaches us to **see challenges as opportunities**, turning empty spaces into places of life and beauty.

Sometimes, the hardest part is just starting. Maybe the soil feels heavy, or you're unsure what to plant first. But guess what? **This book is your gardening buddy**! Together, we'll explore **easy, fun steps to make your gardening adventure unforgettable.** You'll see that gardening is about **progress, not perfection**, and every small effort brings you closer to a thriving garden.

Grow Your Skills, Confidence, and Love for Nature

Gardening is like an adventure, where every step uncovers new treasures and builds your resilience, creativity, and focus. It's about learning to observe the world around you—**noticing how much sunlight plants receive, how plants grow differently in shade or sun, and how insects interact with flowers.** Setbacks, like wilting plants or weeds, aren't just problems— they're opportunities to learn and grow as a gardener!

As you care for your garden, you'll also learn to care for yourself and the planet. Gardening inspires you to think about the environment, create spaces for pollinators, and **embrace**

the role of a steward for the earth. It teaches patience, responsibility, and the satisfaction of nurturing something from a tiny seed into a beautiful bloom.

Let's Get Growing!

Whether you're working with a big backyard, a balcony, or just a sunny windowsill, **this book is packed with tips and activities** to help you grow your garden—and your curiosity. You'll learn how to start your butterfly garden, raise caterpillars, make an insect hotel, and even create tasty recipes using flowers and plants. Every activity is designed to bring out your creativity, build your confidence, and help you **connect with nature on a deeper level.**

By the end, you'll see that gardening isn't just about flowers or plants. It's about growing yourself—your resilience, your caring nature, and your ability to **find joy in the little things, even when the journey takes time.** You're about to discover that with a little love, attention, and creativity, your garden (and you!) will thrive like never before!

In a Hurry?

This book is bursting with fun extras like "Fun Fact," "Think About It," "To Find Out More," "Challenges," and "Did you know?" boxes, which are written in a smaller size. Feel free to breeze past them for now—you can always come back to these fun extras when you have time!

Chapter 1

Discovery of Flowers

Chapter 1 introduces readers to the important parts and amazing functions of flowers, including how they help pollinators. You will learn about annuals, perennials, and biennials, and discover the fun idea of growing plants together to help each other. This chapter highlights how flowers help pollinators, support ecosystems, and contribute to nature in many ways. Get ready for fun activities and challenges that will turn you into a gardening expert! Activities and insights encourage young gardeners to observe, nurture, and connect with plants in meaningful ways.

What is a Flower?

Let's dive into the amazing world of flowers! But first, **what exactly is a flower**? Flowers are one of nature's most beautiful creations, but they're more than just pretty petals. A flower is the part of a plant that makes seeds and fruits, allowing it to create new plants. Imagine it as a tiny factory producing everything needed to grow new plants! The bright colors and unique shapes of flowers

aren't just for decoration—they actually help plants survive by attracting animals like bees, butterflies, and even bats. These creatures help with pollination, the process that allows plants to produce seeds.

Most flowers have special parts like petals, a pistil, and stamens—each playing a role in helping flowers grow and reproduce. Each of these parts plays a role in helping the flower grow and reproduce.

Whether you're spotting a dandelion

> **Fun Fact:** There are over 300,000 types of flowers in the world!

on the sidewalk or growing a colorful marigold, flowers are fascinating because of the variety of shapes, colors, and sizes. They can be as tiny as a pea or larger than a soccer ball! Flowers are truly a wonder of nature and a vital part of our environment—one that you can help protect and enjoy in your own garden!

Did you know? Some flowers only bloom at night! This is the case for the **saguaros** (*Carnegiea gigantea*), known for their night-blooming flowers which often close by midday. These tall cacti bloom at night to attract nocturnal pollinators, such as bats and certain moths, which are active after sunset in their native desert habitats.

Basic Botany Vocabulary

Learning about flowers means learning a bit of botany, which is the study of plants! Here are some of the most important words that will help you understand flowers better:

- **Petals:** These are the colorful, often soft parts of a flower that surround the center. They attract pollinators like bees and butterflies.

- **Stamens:** These parts produce pollen, a powdery substance that helps flowers make seeds when it reaches the pistil.

- **Pistil:** The pistil is the central part of the flower. It contains the ovary, where seeds are made and stored after pollination.

- **Pollen:** This yellow powder helps create seeds to make new plants. Insects like bees transfer pollen from one flower to another.

- **Sepals:** Sepals look like small leaves and are found at the base of a flower. They protect the flower bud before it opens.

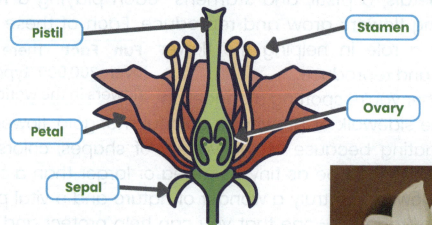

Did you know? Some flowers, like lilies, have extra-large stamens that produce lots of pollen!

With these words in mind, you'll soon see flowers in a new way. Not only are they beautiful, but each part has an important job to help flowers grow and spread seeds!

Now you're ready to look at flowers like a scientist!

Why Are Flowers Important to Nature?

Pollinators and Flowers

Flowers are more than just beautiful —they're vital to nature! One of their main roles is to support animals, especially **pollinators** like bees and butterflies. These creatures collect nectar from flowers for energy. In the

process, they also spread pollen, helping plants make seeds. Without this, many plants couldn't reproduce, and some animals wouldn't have food.

Flowers Support Animals

Beyond pollinators, flowers benefit countless animals. Birds, for instance, eat flower seeds or berries produced after pollination. Small animals use flowers for shelter or to hide from predators. Some insects even hide among flower petals to avoid being seen by predators.

Sparrow with a seed in its beak.

Bug hidden on a leaf.

By caring for flowers, you're helping animals, the air, and the planet!

Flowers and Climate

Flowers even play a role in maintaining the climate. Plants **release oxygen** and absorb carbon dioxide, which helps clean the air.

Like algae in an aquarium, which release oxygen bubbles underwater, plants release oxygen to keep our air clean.

Why Are Flowers Important to Nature?

Food Web Connections

Flowers also support entire ecosystems by creating food chains. When a bee collects nectar, it also collects pollen to bring back to its hive, which eventually becomes honey. Meanwhile, the plant produces seeds that might grow into new flowers or feed other creatures. This process is part of the food web, a big web of connections between all plants, animals, and people.

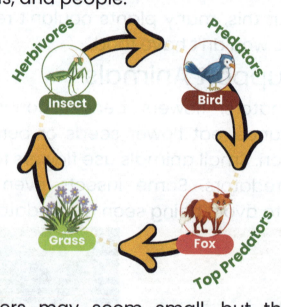

In short, flowers may seem small, but they're mighty heroes in nature! And by planting and caring for them, you can help keep the world thriving!

Flowers don't just connect animals in the food web; they also come in different shapes, colors, and types, each with a unique job in nature. Some flowers live for just one season, while others return year after year, providing pollinators with food across different times of the year. **Let's explore how these different types of flowers contribute to pollination and the natural world.**

Did you know? Some flowers are designed for specific pollinators! Hummingbirds are attracted to red, tubular flowers, while bees love yellow and blue flowers.

The Different Types of Flowers and Their Role in Pollination

Have you ever noticed how different flowers attract different animals? Let's find out why!

Flowers come in many types, each with a unique role in nature, especially when it comes to pollination. **Annuals**, like marigolds and sunflowers, complete their life cycle in one year. They rely on the pollinators they attract during their short, vibrant lives to reproduce. **Perennials**, like daisies and lavender, live for several years and bloom every season, providing pollinators with a reliable food source year after year.

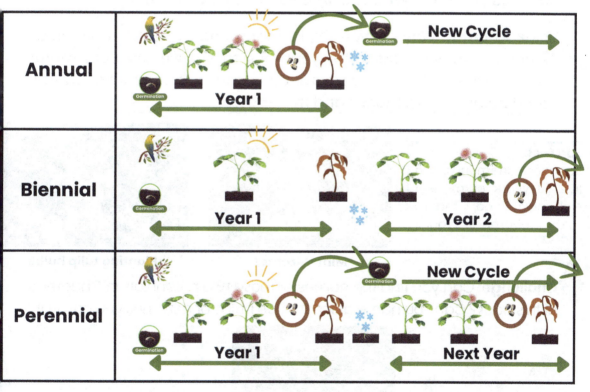

Did you know that some flowers live for just one season, while others return year after year? Each type—annuals, biennials, and perennials—has its own way of growing and supporting pollinators. **Ready to discover what makes each type special and how they help keep nature's cycles in balance?**

What Makes the Difference?

Did you know that among the large number of flowering plant species, three quarter of them are **perennials**? This way, they live for multiple years and often have robust root systems that allow them to survive through various seasons.

Perennials are like marathon runners. They grow big, deep roots that store lots of energy, so they can keep coming back year after year. These roots help them survive through all kinds of weather, even winter. That's why you see some flowers, like daisies or lavender, in gardens every spring!

While *columbines* or *coreopsis*, may live around 3 to 5 years, *purple coneflowers* and *asters* often thrive for 10 to 15 years with proper care. There are long-lived perennials, such as peonies, which can even live decades!

> **Think About It**: Why do you think storing energy in the roots helps perennials survive year after year? It's to survive the cold winter season! These plants have something like a long-lasting battery called bulbs, corms, tubers, and rhizomes.

> **Fun Fact:**
> Japanese anemones, can live 20 years or more if well-maintained, thanks to their rhizome-like roots.

Mint rhizomes

Planting tulip bulbs

Challenge: Can you find the names of these two perennials in Chapter 5 of this book? Can you name at least three bulbs or rhizomes you can eat?

-
-
-

Biennials are like planners. They spend their first year building strong roots and leaves, like getting ready for their big bloom. These roots store energy to help the plant survive the winter and come back strong in the second year to make flowers and seeds.

Parsley roots

Sweet William

Black-eyed Susan

Annual plants are like sprinters racing through the season. They grow really fast, flower, and make seeds all in one season. Since they don't need to survive winter, they only grow small, simple roots. These roots get the plant through its short life, but they don't store extra energy for next year.

Think About It: What do you think is the advantage of having a strong root system that lasts for two years instead of just one?

Annual plant thin roots

Challenge: Can you find the names of these three annuals in Chapter 5 of this book?

As you understood, annuals and biennials are less represented than perennials among the flowering plant species. When perennials can expand thanks to seeding, but still maintain their presence where they already thrive, annuals and biennials only rely on seeding either to keep ground or expand.

Think About It: Why do you think annuals and biennials still exist on Earth? It's probably because when their environment is submitted to strong variations. Both annuals and biennials are focused on producing lots of seeds that can travel to new territories, transported by wind, streams or even animals.

Think About It: What other reasons can you think of for why seeds might travel?

Did you know? *Biennials* often self-seed, creating a natural cycle of first-year and second-year plants in a garden. In a similar manner, *annuals* can reseed themselves which can be nice, as you might still see them again in the next season if they drop seeds!
Have you ever seen a flower grow back on its own?

The Role of Flowers in Pollination

Pollination is essential for these flowers to create seeds. Some flowers rely on the wind to carry their pollen, but most depend on animals, like bees, butterflies, and even birds. **Open flowers** like daisies offer easy pollen access, ideal for bees. **Tube-shaped flowers** like Red cardinal flower attract butterflies and hummingbirds that have long, narrow feeding structures.

The variety of flower shapes, colors, and scents is no accident—each is adapted to attract specific pollinators. Bright, colorful flowers with sweet scents appeal to bees and butterflies, while white or pale flowers that bloom at night attract moths.

Understanding the types of flowers and their role in pollination helps us appreciate how well nature's systems work together. Each flower type not only supports pollinators but also helps sustain the plants, animals, and insects in its environment.
By planting a variety of flowers, you can help provide food for pollinators all season long!

Guide to Companion Plants

Garden Allies, Not Competitors

In the world of plants, some flowers and vegetables grow better together because they don't compete with each other for resources. Instead, they support their neighbors in unique ways. This is called companion planting, where plants work together as allies, not competitors. Each companion plant plays a special role, helping nearby plants by deterring pests, attracting helpful insects, enriching the soil, or providing shade and moisture. Let's explore how these natural friendships can create a healthier and more vibrant garden!

Timing Matters

When choosing companion plants, it's important to consider when each plant blooms or is most active. If a pest-deterring plant, like marigold, only blooms in summer and fall, it might not be as helpful for plants that face pests earlier in the season, like petunia, which starts blooming in May. For the best results, pair plants that bloom around the same time or provide continuous coverage.

Examples of Pest Deterrents

Some plants naturally repel pests, protecting nearby flowers during their growing seasons.

- **Marigold:** Known for deterring soil pests, Marigold blooms from June to October, making it ideal for summer-blooming plants like **petunia, cosmos, and aster**.

Petunia

Cosmos

Aster

More on Pest Deterrents

- **Nasturtium:** This plant, which starts blooming in late spring, acts as a "trap crop" by attracting aphids and protecting plants like **zinnia**, **cosmos**, and **sunflower** through early summer.

Zinnia

Cosmos

Sunflower

Examples of Beneficial Insect Attractors

To attract pollinators or helpful insects, choose flowers that bloom during the same periods as your main plants.

- **Alyssum:** With its long bloom period from early spring to fall, Alyssum can attract hoverflies to help protect plants like **pansy** and **snapdragon.**

Pansy

Snapdragon

- **Borage:** Blooming from early summer, Borage attracts pollinators, supporting **marigolds**, **aster**, and **zinnia** during the peak growing season.

Marigold

Aster

Zinnia

Tip: Check your plants' bloom times to make sure they provide protection or benefits to their neighbors when they need it most!

Examples of Nutrient Enrichers

Some companion plants not only enrich the soil but also provide these benefits throughout their growth cycle, helping neighboring plants thrive.

- **Borage:** Known for its soil-enriching properties, Borage grows through summer, benefiting plants with longer bloom periods like **coreopsis** and **snapdragon**.

Coreopsis   **Snapdragon**

- **Alyssum:** Since it acts as ground cover and decomposes slowly, Alyssum supports **pansy** and **primrose** with moisture and nutrients across the season.

Pansy   **Primrose**

Shade and Soil Moisture Support

For plants that need shelter from the hot sun, choose taller or ground-cover companions that provide shade when needed.

- **Trailing Lobelia:** This plant can help retain moisture in the soil all season long, benefiting **petunia**, **pansy** and **primrose** that thrive in cool, moist soil.

Petunia   **Pansy**   **Primrose**

To Go Further

Think About It: What plant combinations would you create? Think about flowers that could help each other grow! Maybe visit a local nursery and ask which flowers make good friends in the garden!

Explanation of Cross-Pollination

Cross-pollination happens when pollen from one flower reaches the pistil of a different flower of the same species. For example, a bee might visit two different apple trees, helping them to exchange pollen. This exchange allows plants to create seeds with a mix of traits, such as better resistance to pests or stronger growth, making them stronger and better adapted to their environment. Some plants rely entirely on animals like bees or birds for this process.

Role of Flowers in the Food Chain

Flowers play an essential role in the food chain. When bees collect nectar and pollen, they help the flowers produce seeds. These seeds grow into new plants, providing food or shelter for other animals, like birds and squirrels. Each step in the food chain is vital: flowers support the health of plants, animals, and even humans by providing food and habitats for other creatures.

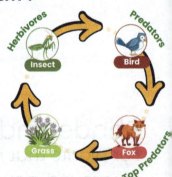

Think About It: What other animals, besides birds and squirrels, might enjoy seeds from flowers? Can you find examples in your garden or local park?

In this way, flowers are more than just a part of the garden; they are vital links in nature's complex food chain. They not only add beauty to our world but also play a critical role in supporting ecosystems. By understanding their importance, we can learn to care for flowers and help the plants, animals, and insects around us thrive together.

Did you know? Some plants can only produce fruit if they're cross-pollinated by bees, birds, or wind. For instance, without cross-pollination, apples and almonds wouldn't grow!

Chapter 2

The Life Cycle of a Plant

This chapter explores the life cycle of plants, starting from seeds germinating to flowering and seed production. It highlights the essential needs of plants, including light, water, and soil, and explains how to improve soil through composting and understanding the nitrogen cycle. The chapter concludes with tips on monitoring plant needs as they grow and how to test soil pH.

From Sowing to Flowering

Discover How Tiny Seeds Transform into Vibrant Blooms!

Every plant begins its journey as a tiny seed, holding all the potential to grow into something beautiful. The life cycle of a plant can be broken down into several stages: **sowing**, **germination**, **growth**, **flowering**, and **seed production**. Understanding these steps helps young gardeners appreciate how plants grow and thrive.

> **Think About It:** Have you ever wondered what makes a seed spring to life when planted in soil?

The cycle starts with a **seed**, which is like a little package filled with nutrients and a tiny plant waiting to sprout. Seeds come in all shapes and sizes—from the tiny, dust-like seeds of petunias to the larger seeds of sunflowers. Each one is a marvel of nature, packed with everything it needs to grow.

- When you plant a seed in soil and give it water, it begins to **germinate**. During this stage, the seed absorbs water, swells, and breaks open.
- A small root, called a **radicle**, grows downward to anchor the plant, while a tiny shoot, called a **plumule**, pushes upward toward the light.

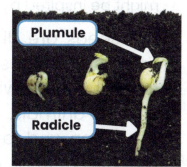

Plumule and radicle come out of the germinating seed.

- The next stage is growth, where the **plant** begins to develop leaves.
- As the plant grows taller and stronger, it begins to prepare for reproduction by forming **buds** that will eventually bloom into **flowers.**

Once the plant reaches the flowering stage, the magic of pollination begins. Have you noticed how flowers invite bees, butterflies and birds? This is how plants call their helpers to carry pollen! And as these creatures carry pollen, they are called **pollinators**. The vibrant petals and sweet scents serve as invitations for pollinators to visit. When pollinators transfer pollen from one flower to another, the plant can create seeds. These seeds are the key to the next generation of plants.

Finally, the plant completes its cycle with seed production.

Think About It: Did you know that the **burdock** plant (*Arctium lappa*) inspired one of the most famous inventions? Swiss engineer George de Mestral noticed how its seeds stuck to his clothes and his dog's fur. This observation led to the creation of Velcro, a fastening system that mimics the plant's tiny hooks! What other inventions might be inspired by nature?

The seeds are dispersed in various ways—some are carried by the wind, others stick to animals, and some are eaten and later spread through animal droppings. Each seed has the potential to start the process all over again.

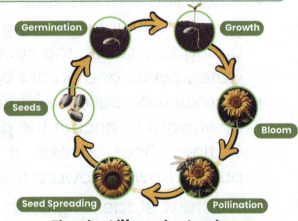

The plant life cycle at a glance.

Watching this cycle is like seeing a plant's adventure unfold—from a tiny seed to a flower that helps the world!

Challenge: Can you spot the annual plants in Chapter 5 of this book? Look for the logo in the detailed descriptions of plants.

The Different Needs of Plants

Plants are like little green chefs—they need the right ingredients to grow: light, water, and soil! Each plant is unique, and understanding these needs ensures they grow healthy and strong.

Light: A Plant's Power Source ☀️

Plants turn sunlight into food through photosynthesis—it's their superpower! Some plants love basking in full sunlight, like sunflowers, while others prefer shady spots, like ferns. Knowing how much light a plant needs helps you decide where to plant it in your garden.

Sunflowers need bright sunlight.

Ferns enjoy cozy shade.

Think About It: Which spot in your garden gets the most sunlight during the day? Which plants might love soaking in that light?

Your Plant Selection Guide in this book, helps you identify how much sunlight the listed plants need using these symbols:

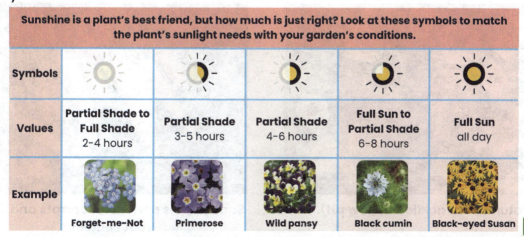

Sunshine is a plant's best friend, but how much is just right? Look at these symbols to match the plant's sunlight needs with your garden's conditions.

Symbols					
Values	Partial Shade to Full Shade 2-4 hours	Partial Shade 3-5 hours	Partial Shade 4-6 hours	Full Sun to Partial Shade 6-8 hours	Full Sun all day
Example	Forget-me-Not	Primerose	Wild pansy	Black cumin	Black-eyed Susan

Water: The Lifeline of Plants

Water is another essential. Plants absorb water through their roots, and then moves up the stem to the leaves and flowers. While too much water can drown plants, too little causes them to wilt. While certain plants, like marigolds, require frequent watering, others, like cacti, require very little.

Cacti need very little water, as they store water for long periods in their roots.

Marigolds love a daily drink!

Soil: A Plant's Home

Fun Fact: Earthworms in the soil help plants by making tiny tunnels that bring air and water to the roots!

Rich, crumbly soil is like a comfy bed for roots. Soil acts like a home for plants. It provides nutrients and anchors roots. The best soil is rich and crumbly, allowing roots to breathe. Some plants need specific soil types—acidic, sandy, or loamy. Adding compost or fertilizer can improve soil quality, giving plants the extra nutrients they need to flourish.

Petunia love acidic soil (low pH).

Sandy soil is perfect for carrots and other root veggies.

Improving your soil ensures every plant gets the nutrients it needs.

Challenge: Observe your garden and check the soil. Is it sandy, loamy, or clay-like? Can you make a plan to improve your garden soil? Think about compost, mulch, or natural fertilizers!

When you match plants with their perfect needs, your garden will thrive beautifully!

Types of Soils and How to Improve them

Every garden starts with soil. The type of soil in your garden determines how well your plants grow. Loamy, clay, and sandy soil are the three main types. Each has unique characteristics, and knowing your soil type helps you improve it to meet your plants' needs.

Sandy Soil: Quick to Drain

Sandy soil feels gritty and allows water to drain quickly. It's

ideal for plants like **cosmos** and **California poppy**, which prefer drier conditions. However, sandy soil can dry out too fast for other plants. Adding **compost**, **shredded leaves**, or other **organic matter** helps sandy soil retain moisture and nutrients.

Cosmos thrive in sandy soil.

Clay Soil: Heavy and Compact

Clay soil is dense and holds water well, but it can become compacted, making it hard for roots to grow. This type of soil works for plants like **pansy** and **wild pansy**, which enjoy moisture, but it needs improvement for better drainage. Mixing in **sand, perlite**, or **gypsum** loosens clay soil and improves air circulation.

Pansies grow well in clay soil.

Black-Eyed Susans prefer a loamy soil.

Loamy Soil: The Gardener's Dream

Loamy soil is a balanced mix of **sand**, **silt**, and **clay**. It feels crumbly and holds water without becoming waterlogged, making it perfect for most plants. If you're lucky enough to have loamy soil, your garden will thrive with minimal effort.

Think About It: What type of soil do you think your garden has? How does it feel when you touch it?

Tips for Improving Your Soil

Improving soil involves adding **organic matter** like:

- **Compost:** Enriches the soil with nutrients.
- **Shredded leaves:** Helps retain moisture.
- **Manure:** Provides essential minerals for plant growth.

You can also test your soil's **pH** to ensure it matches your plants' preferences:

- **Acidic** soil is ideal for plants like **black cumin**.
- **Alkaline** soil suits plants like **Mexican fleabane**.

By understanding and improving your soil, you build a strong foundation for your garden. Healthy soil means healthy plants!

Think About It: Which of these soil improvement methods would you like to try in your garden?

Did you know? Moles are insectivores: they eat insects, worms, and even grubs! While their tunnels might disturb roots, they also aerate the soil, improving drainage and helping plant roots access air and water.

When you care for your soil, you're caring for your entire garden ecosystem.

The Nitrogen Cycle and Plant Growth

Nitrogen: A Key to Plant Growth

Nitrogen is one of the most important nutrients for plants. It supports the development of robust stems, lush foliage, and vibrant flowers. Without nitrogen, plants would struggle to grow and thrive.

Why Plants Love Nitrogen

In nature, nitrogen is all around us—it's in the air! But plants can't absorb nitrogen directly from the air. That's where the nitrogen cycle comes in. Tiny organisms in the soil, called nitrogen-fixing bacteria, transform nitrogen gas into a form that plants can use. These helpful bacteria work like tiny chefs, preparing nitrogen "meals" that plants absorb through their roots.

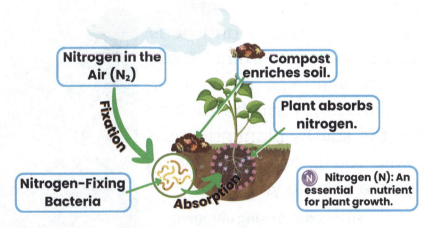

How plants get nitrogen.

The nitrogen cycle helps plants grow by turning air into food-friendly nutrients!

This natural process enriches the soil, creating a sustainable nutrient supply. It's an amazing partnership between plants and soil microbes that keeps gardens healthy and thriving.

Healthy soil, happy plants—let nitrogen work its magic!

Boosting Nitrogen in Your Garden

How to Keep Your Soil Nitrogen-Rich

Understanding the nitrogen cycle can help you give your plants exactly what they need to grow strong and healthy. Here are some ways to boost nitrogen in your soil:

1. Use Compost and Fertilizers

Compost is a great way to recycle kitchen scraps and garden waste into valuable nutrients for your plants. Grass clippings, shredded leaves, and manure are also rich sources of nitrogen. These organic materials break down in the soil, feeding plants over time.

2. Grow Nitrogen-Fixing Plants

Some plants, like beans and peas, are natural nitrogen-fixers. These plants work with soil bacteria to capture nitrogen from the air and add it to the soil. By planting beans and peas, you're not just growing food—you're helping your soil!

Root nodules fixing nitrogen.

Did you know? Beans and peas have tiny nodules on their roots where nitrogen-fixing bacteria live. These bacteria work hard to capture nitrogen from the air and share it with the plant!

Challenge: Can you think of ways to recycle kitchen scraps into compost for your garden? What plants in your garden might benefit from extra nitrogen?

Avoiding Too Much Nitrogen

While nitrogen is essential, too much of it can cause problems. Plants may grow lots of leaves but produce fewer flowers. That's why balance is key—use nitrogen-rich compost wisely and observe how your plants respond.

Tip: Grass clippings from lawn mower robots make an excellent natural fertilizer! Spread them thinly in your garden to provide nutrients and keep the soil healthy.

Too much nitrogen can lead to lots of leaves but fewer—and sometimes less vibrant—flowers!

Finding the right nitrogen balance is key to growing healthy and blooming plants!

Did you know? Signs of too much nitrogen include overly green, leafy plants with weak or no flowers. Check your plants regularly to keep the balance!

How Plant Needs Change Over Time

Plants, like people, have different needs as they grow. By observing these changes, gardeners can give plants the care they need to thrive at every stage.

Seedlings need frequent watering to stay moist but not soggy!

> **Tip:** Use a spray bottle to gently water seedlings without disturbing the soil.

Caring for Young Seedlings

Young seedlings are like babies—they're delicate and need extra attention! Their roots are shallow, so they require frequent watering to keep the soil moist. Be careful not to overwater, as soggy soil can cause root rot. At this stage, gentle handling and regular monitoring are key to healthy growth.

Meeting the Needs of Mature Plants

As **plants mature**, their roots grow deeper into the soil, making them better at finding water and nutrients. Plants like cosmos adapt well to needing less water as they mature, making them resilient in diverse conditions. Their nutrient requirements, however, increase during flowering and fruiting. Adding compost or fertilizers at this stage supports their growth and productivity.

**Sunflowers send roots deep
into the soil to find water.**

Fun Fact: Some mature plants, like sunflowers, can send roots as deep as 6 feet to find water!

Did you know? As plants grow, their light needs change too—let's find out how!

How Plants Find Their Perfect Light!

Light needs can also change as plants grow. Seedlings often thrive in full sun to fuel their rapid growth, but as plants get larger, some may benefit from partial shade to avoid overheating. Observing your plants and adjusting their environment helps keep them healthy through every stage.

To Go Further

The Science of Photosynthesis

Plants are like tiny factories! They use **sunlight, water, and carbon dioxide** to create their food through a process called **photosynthesis**. This amazing transformation produces **glucose**, the energy plants need to grow, and **oxygen**, which is released into the air. Without photosynthesis, plants—and life as we know it—couldn't exist!

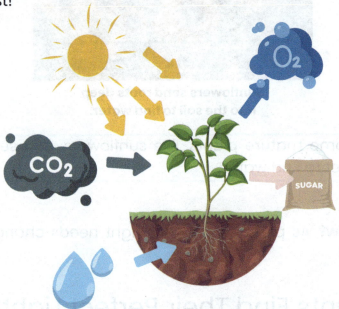

Leaves produce oxygen and sugar.

Did you know? Trees and plants are sometimes called the "lungs of the Earth" because they release oxygen and absorb carbon dioxide, keeping the air clean and breathable.

Composting: Nature's Recycling

Did you know you can turn your kitchen scraps into "black gold" for your garden? Composting is a natural process that breaks down banana peels, fruit peels, apple cores, grass clippings, and leaves into nutrient-rich compost. Adding compost to your garden improves the soil, helping plants grow healthy and strong.

> **Tip:** Think of compost as your garden's menu—only add what plants love to "eat"! Avoid adding meat, dairy, or oily foods. These items take longer to break down and can attract pests. To speed up composting, chop large items like banana peels into smaller pieces and mix them in your compost pile.

Once your compost is ready, it adds nutrients to your soil. But what nutrients do plants need most? Let's find out!

Challenge: Can you create your own mini-compost bin? Try collecting fruit peels, vegetable scraps, and dried leaves for a few weeks. Watch how they transform into compost you can use in your garden!

The Big Three Nutrients: N-P-K

Plants need three key nutrients to thrive:
- **Nitrogen (N):** Encourages leafy growth.
- **Phosphorus (P):** Develops strong roots.
- **Potassium (K):** Promotes flowers and fruits.

Testing your soil helps identify which nutrients are missing, so you can use organic fertilizers like bone meal, compost tea, or wood ash to keep plants happy and healthy.

How Can You Test for Nutrients?

Testing soil nutrients might sound tricky, but here's an easy way to get started:

1. DIY Soil Observation
- **Nitrogen Deficiency:** Look for yellow leaves or slow growth. Plants need nitrogen for green, leafy stems.
- **Phosphorus Deficiency:** Check for purple or reddish leaves and weak root systems. Phosphorus is essential for strong roots!
- **Potassium Deficiency:** Watch for browning or curling leaf edges. Potassium helps with flowering and fruiting.

2. Plant Clues
- Experiment by planting a leafy vegetable like lettuce, a root vegetable like carrots, and a flowering plant like zinnias. Observe their growth. Uneven growth might mean the soil lacks specific nutrients.

3. Store-Bought Test Kits
- Simple test kits are available at garden stores. They include color-coded capsules for each nutrient. Just follow the instructions to see if your soil needs extra nutrients.

Why It Matters: Healthy soil supports healthy plants. By testing and adding the right nutrients, you help your garden bloom and thrive!

Challenge: Can you identify signs of nutrient deficiencies in your garden? Compare leaves, roots, and flowers to see which plants are happiest!

Check Your Soil's pH: A Simple Experiment

What is pH?

pH is a scale from **0 to 14** that tells us how "acidic" or "alkaline" something is:

- **Neutral soil** (pH 7) is just like pure water and is perfect for growing most vegetables, like lettuce.
- **Acidic soil** (low pH, below 7) is great for plants like petunias.
- **Alkaline soil** (high pH, above 7) suits plants like wallflower.

Most plants grow best in **neutral or slightly acidic soil**. Knowing your soil's pH helps you choose the right plants or decide if your soil needs adjustments.

 Make sure to **work with an adult** while handling **vinegar** or **baking soda**!

Knowing your soil's health is like checking its energy levels! With a few simple steps, you can discover important details about your garden soil—no fancy tools needed! Here's how:

1. Collect Some Soil: Take a small scoop of soil from your garden. Divide it into two small bowls or cups for testing.

2. DIY pH Test (Vinegar and Baking Soda):

- **What You Need:** Vinegar, baking soda, water, and your soil samples.
- **Steps:**
    - Add a tablespoon of soil to the first cup and pour a small amount of vinegar over it. If it fizzes, your soil is **alkaline**.
    - Mix a tablespoon of soil with water in the second cup until it's muddy. Sprinkle baking soda on top. If it fizzes, your soil is **acidic**.
    - If neither reacts, your soil is likely **neutral**—perfect for most plants!
- **Why It Matters:** Knowing your soil's pH helps you decide which plants will grow best and if nutrients need to be added.

3. Optional pH Test Kit: You can also use a soil pH test kit from a garden store. It's like a mini science experiment and gives more precise results. Just follow the instructions!

4. Observe the Soil: Look at its texture and color. Is it sandy, sticky (clay-like), or crumbly (loamy)? Loamy soil is the best for most plants because it holds water while still draining well.

Once you know your soil's pH, you can choose the perfect plants for your garden or add compost to balance it! Try grouping your garden plants by their pH preferences and observe which ones thrive!

Did you know? Worms in your garden are a great sign of healthy soil! Worms help mix the soil and create tiny air tunnels, making it perfect for plant roots.

Chapter 3

Starting Your Butterfly Garden

In Chapter 3, you will learn about the best planting techniques, soil preparation, seasonal flower choices, and gardening safety. It offers practical advice for indoor and outdoor planting, soil improvement, and creative ways to grow flowers all year long while emphasizing safety tips for young gardeners.

When and Where to Plant

Timing is everything when starting your butterfly garden! Most flowers thrive when planted in spring, as the warming soil and longer days create perfect conditions for growth. But some hardy flowers, like pansies or primroses, enjoy cooler months and can be planted earlier.

Indoor Planting

For a head start, plant indoors! Sow seeds in small pots or trays 6 to 8 weeks before the last frost. Place them by a sunny window or under a grow light for plenty of light. Once the weather warms, you can carefully transplant them to your garden.

> **Tip:** Start with seed trays labeled with the plant names so you remember what you planted!

Decorate your seed labels with butterflies or flowers for a personal touch!

Now your indoor plants are thriving and are ready for the adventure of outdoor life!

Outdoor Planting, Climate Considerations

Your outdoor planting schedule depends on your region's climate. In areas with mild winters, you can plant seeds directly in late winter. In colder regions, wait until the soil has thawed and warmed enough for seeds to germinate.

Remember to check your seed packets for specific instructions—they're like little guides for when and where to plant each flower. Careful planning ensures your butterfly garden will flourish and provide a welcoming space for pollinators to visit.

Consider using weather apps or check local gardening resources to track frost dates!

Think About It: What flowers grow best in your region during spring and summer? Could you mix early and late bloomers to keep your garden colorful for longer? Imagine how vibrant your garden could look with flowers blooming all season long!

With careful planning, your butterfly garden will be a vibrant haven, ready to welcome these fluttering beauties!

Prepare Your Soil for a Healthy Garden

Why Soil Matters

Healthy soil is the foundation of any garden, especially a butterfly garden. It provides the nutrients and structure plants need to grow strong and attract pollinators. Without well-prepared soil, plants may struggle to thrive, and your garden won't reach its full potential. The good news? A little preparation can make all the difference!

Did you know? A single teaspoon of healthy soil can contain more microbes than there are people on Earth!

Testing Your Soil: Find the Perfect Balance

Start by testing your soil. A simple soil test kit can tell you its pH level and nutrient content. Most flowers prefer slightly acidic to neutral soil (pH 6.0–7.0). If your soil is too acidic, adding lime can help. If it's too alkaline, sulfur or organic compost can bring it back into balance. Not sure how to check your soil's pH? Turn back to **Chapter 2** for an easy vinegar-and-baking-soda experiment to test it at home! Testing ensures your garden has the right foundation for beautiful blooms.

> **Tip:** You can use crushed eggshells to add calcium to your soil and help balance its pH!

Now that you've tested your soil, let's explore how to improve its texture and nutrients for thriving plants!

How to Improve Your Soil

Loosen and Aerate Your Soil

Before you start planting, use a garden fork or tiller to loosen the soil. This step improves drainage, allows roots to grow freely, and prevents water from pooling—an issue that can lead to root rot. Well-aerated soil is like a breath of fresh air for your plants!

Think About It: What's the texture of your garden soil? Is it sandy, sticky, or crumbly? How can you improve it for healthier plants?

Adjust Your Soil's Texture

Is your soil clay-heavy? Mix in sand or organic matter to improve its structure and prevent it from becoming compacted. If it's sandy, add compost to help retain moisture and nutrients. The goal is crumbly, well-draining soil that feels just right in your hands.

Boost Nutrients with Compost and Mulch

Adding a 2–3 inch layer of organic amendments like compost or well-rotted manure enriches the soil with essential nutrients. Mulch on top of the soil keeps it moist, regulates temperature, and protects roots from the summer heat. This combo creates the perfect growing conditions for your butterfly-friendly plants.

Even if your garden soil isn't perfect, raised beds and containers can help you create the ideal environment for your butterfly plants!

What If Your Soil Isn't Perfect?

Why Choose Raised Beds?

If your soil is poor, raised beds can save the day! They allow you to control soil quality, improve drainage, and keep weeds at bay. Raised beds also warm up faster in spring, giving your butterfly garden an early start. Plus, they're great for kids because they're easier to reach!

A bed that's about 4 feet wide is perfect for easy access.

Did you know? Some fungi, called mycorrhizae, form partnerships with plant roots! They help plants absorb nutrients like phosphorus and water, while the plants share sugars they produce through photosynthesis. It's like nature's teamwork underground!

Container Gardening: Perfect for Small Spaces

No space for a garden? No problem! Containers let you grow butterfly-friendly plants almost anywhere. Use lightweight soil mixes for easy drainage, and be sure to place your pots in sunny spots. You can even move them around to catch the best light!

Tip: Use lightweight soil mix in containers for easy drainage and healthy root growth!

Sowing Seeds for a Thriving Garden

Planting seeds is an exciting start to your gardening journey—it's like planting little promises that will bloom into beauty! Did you know there are different ways to sow seeds, and each works best for specific garden styles and flower types?

Broadcast Sowing

Broadcast sowing is a simple and natural method. Scatter seeds evenly across the soil surface, just like sprinkling confetti—imagine you're throwing a garden party! This method is perfect for creating wildflower meadows or free-flowing gardens. After scattering, gently rake the soil to lightly cover the seeds and water the area. Watch your seeds grow into a colorful paradise for pollinators!

Scattering seeds to create a natural masterpiece.

Tip: Try broadcast sowing in bare patches of your garden during spring to attract butterflies and bees!

Row Planting

Row planting is perfect for gardeners who love structure and neatness. Use a stick or hoe to draw straight, shallow furrows in the soil. Place the seeds evenly in the rows, following the spacing instructions on the seed packet. Cover the seeds with a thin layer of soil and water them gently to settle them in place. This method works beautifully for vegetables and flowers like zinnias or cosmos, creating tidy rows that are easy to care for!

Individual Planting

Individual planting is the best choice for larger seeds, such as sunflowers or nasturtiums. Dig small holes at the recommended depth and drop a single seed into each. Cover the seeds with soil and water lightly. This method ensures that each plant has plenty of space to grow strong and healthy.

Prefer individual planting for larger seeds like sunflowers.

Sowing Secrets for Success

Whichever sowing method you choose, these handy tips will help your garden thrive!

- **Planting Depth:** Follow the seed packet's advice for planting depth—too deep or shallow can prevent seeds from sprouting.
- **Spacing:** Give your plants room to grow by following the spacing guide on the seed packet.
- **Watering:** Water gently to keep the soil moist (not soggy!) and prevent seeds from washing away.
- **Sunlight:** Make sure your seeds get enough sunlight—check if they need full sun, partial shade, or shade.
- **Label Your Seeds:** Mark where each seed is planted with labels so you'll remember what's growing where!

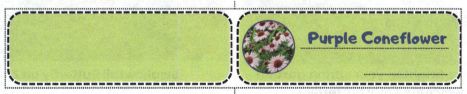

Create and print your own labels or purchase them from a local nurserey.

Did you know? Seeds carry their own food reserves! These provide energy until the first leaves emerge to collect sunlight.

With the right techniques, your garden will soon bloom— ready to welcome butterflies and pollinators!

Choosing Flowers for Every Season

Planning seasonal blooms keeps your butterfly garden lively, vivid, and full of life year-round! Each season brings unique blooms that provide nectar for butterflies and color for your garden. With careful planning, you can create a thriving haven that's beautiful in every season!

Spring Blooms: A Fresh Start

Spring marks a fresh start, with flowers like pansies, columbines, and forget-me-nots thriving in the cool weather. These blooms provide early nectar for butterflies emerging from hibernation, bringing vibrant life to your garden as winter fades.

Summer: Sun-Loving Blooms

Summer bursts with bold, sun-loving flowers like sunflowers, zinnias, and cosmos. These vibrant blooms provide abundant nectar for butterflies and thrive in the warm sunshine, ensuring your garden is bursting with vibrant colors during the longest days of the year.

What's your favorite summer flower—sunflowers, zinnias, or cosmos? They're all butterfly favorites!

Columbines brighten your spring garden and welcome early butterflies.

Swallowtail Butterfly on Zinnia.

Tip: Plant sunflowers by a sunny fence or wall to attract butterflies and birds!

Autumn Colors: Late Blooms

Autumn flowers, like asters and marigolds, bloom well into

fall offers essential nectar for butterflies preparing for migration or overwintering. Their warm hues reflect the beauty of the season and keep late-season pollinators visiting.

Did you know? Monarch butterflies depend on fall flowers like asters to fuel their incredible 3,000-mile migrations. Could your garden be part of their journey?

Winter Wonders: Hardy Blooms

In milder climates, winter blooms like hellebores and cyclamens bring beauty to chilly days. These hardy flowers brighten frosty days, keeping your garden vibrant even during winter's chill.

A monarch resting on asters during migration season.

Cyclamens with frost on their leaves— beauty in every season.

Think About It: What flowers could you add to your garden to create color and nectar in the winter? Research online or ask a local nursery about hardy plants for winter in your region.

By choosing flowers that bloom in every season, you provide a year-round buffet for butterflies and create a garden that's always buzzing with life. A little planning goes a long way to ensure your garden remains vibrant, colorful, and pollinator-friendly.

Start planning your seasonal flowers today and create a garden that's always buzzing with life!

Ready to make your garden safe for all its visitors? Let's talk about general garden safety tips!

Garden Safely and Have Fun!

Gardening is an amazing way to explore nature and have fun, but safety should always come first. With a few simple precautions, young gardeners can enjoy their butterfly garden safely and confidently!

Protect Your Hands

Gardening gloves are a gardener's best friend! They protect your hands from sharp tools, thorny plants, and potentially harmful substances like fertilizers or pesticides. Gloves also prevent skin irritation from certain plants, so always slip them on before digging into the soil!

Did you know? Gloves aren't just for safety—they also keep your hands clean so you can enjoy a snack after gardening without a big clean-up!

Watch Out for Toxic Plants

Some flowers, like marigolds or cyclamens, might irritate the skin or be harmful if eaten. Teach young gardeners to identify these plants and handle them with care. It's also a good idea to learn which flowers are safe for butterflies but not for curious pets!

Think About It: Can you research which plants are safe for your region? Browse the plant list in this book—some are mildly toxic and need careful handling. Create a garden safety list to help you, your family, and your pets enjoy your butterfly garden worry-free!

Plants like Japanese anemones or cyclamens are marked as toxic in this book.

Practice Good Hygiene

After gardening, always wash your hands with soap and

water, especially if you've been handling soil or plants. This helps prevent the spread of germs or harmful bacteria. And remember—avoid touching your eyes, mouth, or face while gardening to stay extra safe!

Use Tools Properly

Gardening tools can make planting fun and easy, but they must be used with care. Always point sharp edges away from your body and store tools safely after use. Teach young gardeners how to handle tools properly, so they can dig and plant like pros!

Appropriate outfit is recommended for gardening.

Tip: Choose lightweight, sized appropriate tools for young gardeners—they're easier to handle and safer to use!

By following these safety tips, you'll enjoy every moment in your garden without worry. Gardening is a safe, rewarding way to connect with nature and create a butterfly-friendly paradise!

With your safety gear ready, it's time to explore a common gardening question: Are weeds pesky intruders or helpful allies? Let's find out in the next chapter!

Enjoying the Book?
We'd Love to Hear Your Thoughts!

We hope you're having fun learning about butterfly gardening!

If this book has **inspired you**, a quick review would mean the world to us. Your feedback **helps other young gardeners** discover this book and supports **independent authors like me!**

💬 **What's your favorite part so far?**
Your thoughts help grow our **community of young Earth Heroes!**

📲 Scan the QR code opposite to leave a short review on Amazon. It only takes **2 minutes,** but it makes a huge impact!

Thank you for being part of this gardening adventure!

Chapter 4

Weeds: Friends or Foes?

In Chapter 4, you'll explore the concept of weeds, discovering how to classify them into annual, biennial, and perennial types. While weeds are often considered a nuisance, some offer surprising benefits like improving soil health and supporting pollinators. You'll also learn to identify helpful weeds like clover and milkweed and try eco-friendly weed control methods, including mulching, hand-pulling, and companion planting. This chapter highlights how balancing weed management supports a thriving garden ecosystem.

Understanding Weeds: Types and Traits

Weeds are often seen as villains in the garden because they compete with flowers for sunlight, water, and nutrients. But are they always bad? While some weeds steal resources from your plants, others can actually improve your garden's health! By understanding the different types of weeds, you'll learn to tell which ones are friends and which are foes.

The Three Types of Weeds

- **Annual Weeds:** These quick growers, like crabgrass, sprout, flower, and spread seeds all in one year. They're easy to pull because of their shallow roots.

Crabgrass: A common annual weed.

- **Biennial Weeds:** Plants like burdock live for two years—producing leaves the first year and flowers and seeds in the second.

Burdock: Has become invasive.

- **Perennial Weeds:** Long-lasting weeds like dandelions return every year, thanks to their deep roots and underground stems.

Dandelions: A well known perennial.

Did you know? Some weeds are edible! Dandelions aren't just weeds—they're one of the first flowers to bloom in spring, feeding hungry bees and butterflies! And their leaves, rich in vitamins, make a tasty salad, and their roots can be roasted for tea. Dandelion roots are also known for their medicinal properties.

Benefits of Unexpected Weeds

Not all weeds are enemies of the garden! In fact, many so-called 'weeds' are actually helpful to the garden and its visitors. Clover improves soil health by fixing nitrogen, while dandelions provide an important early source of nectar for pollinators when other flowers are scarce. Plantain helps break up compacted soil, and yarrow offers shelter to beneficial insects like ladybugs.

A bee and a butterfly eating on clover.

A ladybug crowling on yarrow.

Weed name	Helpful
Dandelion	✔️
Bramble	❌

Weeds or Allies? A Mini Guide

- **Dandelion:** Its sunny yellow flowers provide early nectar for pollinators, and its leaves and roots are edible.

- **Plantain:** This low-growing plant improves soil health and provides food for butterfly caterpillars.

- **Milkweed:** Essential for monarch butterflies, milkweed offers nectar-rich flowers and leaves that monarch caterpillars rely on for food.

- **Clover:** Often mistaken for a weed, clover fixes nitrogen in the soil and attracts bees and butterflies to your garden.

Eco-Friendly Weed Control Tips

Controlling weeds doesn't have to mean using harmful chemicals. Here are four natural and eco-friendly ways to keep weeds in check:

- **Mulching:** A layer of mulch blocks sunlight, prevents weeds from sprouting, and adds nutrients as it breaks down.
- **Hand Pulling:** Pulling weeds by hand is most effective after rain, when the soil is soft and roots come out easily.
- **Smothering:** Covering the ground with cardboard or newspaper blocks sunlight, preventing weeds from growing. Add mulch on top for a finished look.
- **Companion Planting:** Some flowers, like marigolds, naturally deter weeds by shading the soil or releasing chemicals that stop weed growth.

By embracing natural methods, you'll support pollinators and keep your garden chemical-free!

Start planning which weeds to let grow and which ones to control. Share your discoveries with your family!

Mulching blocks sunlight and prevents weeds naturally!

Hand clean the area around your plants.

> **Tip:** Mulching not only prevents weeds but also keeps the soil cool and moist during hot summer days!

Balancing Nature and Control

Managing weeds doesn't mean removing them all. Some weeds can benefit your garden, while others need careful control. By using natural methods and learning to recognize helpful plants, you can maintain a garden that's healthy, beautiful, and butterfly-friendly!

> **Fun Fact:** The roots of dandelions can grow up to 15 feet deep, making them some of the most resilient plants in the world!

By learning to identify weeds and understanding their role in the garden, you're already on your way to becoming a butterfly garden expert! Some "weeds" may even surprise you by their ability to support pollinators and improve the soil. With your newfound knowledge, it's time to shift focus to the plants you'll want to nurture. Let's explore 36 amazing plants that will transform your garden into a butterfly haven!

> **Think About It:** What other natural methods can you find to control weeds? Discuss with your family!

**With your new weed wisdom, you're ready to choose plants that complement your garden.
Let's discover 36 wonderful plants to nurture!**

Chapter 5

Plant Selection Guide

Chapter 5 introduces 36 unique flowers that are perfect for a butterfly-friendly garden. You'll begin by exploring key gardening concepts such as hardiness zones, seasonal flower planning, and the importance of "Friendly Neighbor Flowers." Symbols are explained in detail to help you understand each flower's needs for sun, water, and care.

This chapter also dives into fascinating details about plant interactions with pollinators and highlights special properties like toxicity or edibility. Finally, it features 36 descriptive profiles, each showcasing one flower's unique personality, starting with Petunia on page 75. These profiles provide all the information young gardeners need to create a colorful and thriving garden.

Introduction

Discover 36 Amazing Flowers!

Hey there, young gardener! Are you excited to meet the plants that will turn your garden into a colorful paradise buzzing with bees, butterflies, and other friendly visitors? In this chapter, you'll get to know flowers with unique "personalities."

Each plant has its own needs—some love soaking up the sun, while others prefer shade. Some need lots of water, while others are happy with just a sip. You'll discover fun facts, like how tall they grow, when they bloom, and which ones suit your garden's climate!

To help you out, we've added handy symbols for things like sunlight, water, and height. And here's a tip: the background color of each page matches the season, so you can tell when it's the best time to plant!

Before diving into each plant's story, check out the lists of flowers by season and meet some "Friendly Neighbors" that grow especially well together. Mixing certain plants can make your garden even livelier!

Ready to start this floral adventure and find the perfect flowers for your dream garden? **Let's go!**

Understanding Hardiness Zones

What's a Hardiness Zone?

A Hardiness Zone is a region defined by the coldest temperatures. Knowing your Hardiness Zone helps you choose plants suited to your garden's climate.

Do you know which Hardiness Zone you live in? Finding out is like solving a fun mystery that helps your plants grow better!

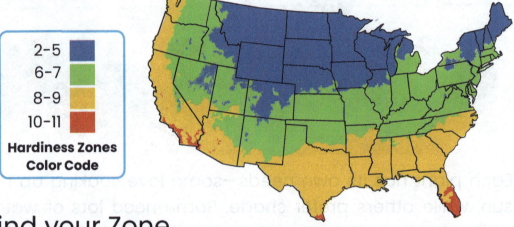

2–5
6–7
8–9
10–11

Hardiness Zones Color Code

Find your Zone

To discover your zone, the USDA* Hardiness Zone Map is a great tool for this! You can find an interactive map online or download maps that show you the zones. Ask an adult to help you search for "USDA Hardiness Zone Map" online to get started. And you know what? There is much more than the interactive Hardiness Zone Map to discover on the USDA website. There is a very detailed plant database where you can learn a lot!

Choose the Right Plants

Once you know your zone, pick plants that are recommended for that temperature range. This gives your green friends the best chance to grow strong and healthy.

Tip: Check if your favorite flowers can grow in your zone!

*United States Department of Agriculture

Link to USDA Plant Hardiness Zones

Which Plants Thrive in My Zone?

The table below lists the plants described in this book and thriving in your Zone.

2-5	Pansy (p. 77), Primrose (p. 78), Columbine (p. 80), Cardinal Flower (p. 81), Aster (p. 82), Wild Pansy (p. 83), Coreopsis (p. 84), Black-eyed Susan (p. 85), Purple Coneflower (p. 87), Zinnia (p. 88), Pot Marigold (p. 89), Cosmos (p. 90), Marigold (p. 91), Alyssum (p. 92), Black Cumin (p. 93), Sunflower (p. 94), Borage (p. 95), Horned Violet (p. 98), Bachelor's Button (p. 99), Sweet William (p. 100), Cyclamen (p. 102), Decorative Cabbage (p. 103), Forget-me-not (p. 105), Peony Poppy (p. 107), Wild Chamomile (p. 108), Virginia Bluebell (p. 109), Japanese Anemone (p. 110)
6-7	Pansy (p. 77), Primrose (p. 78), Columbine (p. 80), Cardinal Flower (p. 81), Aster (p. 82), Wild Pansy (p. 83), Coreopsis (p. 84), Black-eyed Susan (p. 85), Purple Coneflower (p. 87), Zinnia (p. 88), Pot Marigold (p. 89), Cosmos (p. 90), Marigold (p. 91), Alyssum (p. 92), Black Cumin (p. 93), Sunflower (p. 94), Borage (p. 95), Snapdragon (p. 97), Horned Violet (p. 98), Bachelor's Button (p. 99), Sweet William (p. 100), Wallflower (p. 101), Cyclamen (p. 102), Decorative Cabbage (p. 103), Forget-me-not (p. 105), Mexican Fleabane (p. 104), California Poppy (p. 106), Peony Poppy (p. 107), Wild Chamomile (p. 108), Virginia Bluebell (p. 109), Japanese Anemone (p. 110)
8-9	Pansy (p. 77), Primrose (p. 78), Columbine (p. 80), Cardinal Flower (p. 81), Aster (p. 82), Wild Pansy (p. 83), Coreopsis (p. 84), Black-eyed Susan (p. 85), Nasturtium (p. 86), Purple Coneflower (p. 87), Zinnia (p. 88), Pot Marigold (p. 89), Cosmos (p. 90), Marigold (p. 91), Alyssum (p. 92), Black Cumin (p. 93), Sunflower (p. 94), Borage (p. 95), Snapdragon (p. 97), Horned Violet (p. 98), Bachelor's Button (p. 99), Sweet William (p. 100), Wallflower (p. 101), Cyclamen (p. 102), Decorative Cabbage (p. 103), Forget-me-not (p. 105), Mexican Fleabane (p. 104), California Poppy (p. 106), Peony Poppy (p. 107), Wild Chamomile (p. 108), Virginia Bluebell (p. 109), Japanese Anemone (p. 110)
10-11	Petunia (p. 75), Salvia (p. 76), Trailing Lobelia (p. 79), Nasturtium (p. 86), Zinnia (p. 88), Pot Marigold (p. 89), Cosmos (p. 90), Marigold (p. 91), Black Cumin (p. 93), Sunflower (p. 94), Borage (p. 95), Spider Flower (p. 96), Snapdragon (p. 97), Bachelor's Button (p. 99), Decorative Cabbage (p. 103), California Poppy (p. 106)

Choose Your Plant Friends!

Are you Ready to Go?

There is always something fun to do in your garden all year round. It could be things like caring plants, observing how they grow, spying which small animals or insects are visiting your plants.

Would you like to try and sow a new plant friend? Let's discover which plants are perfect for each season!

Want to know what you can sow now? Let's check it out! And don't worry, you'll find more detailed descriptions just ahead.

This outline shows the season, here it's winter.

For each suggested plant, that's the the months you can sow indoors or outdoors...

... and when it typically blooms and give colors to your garden!

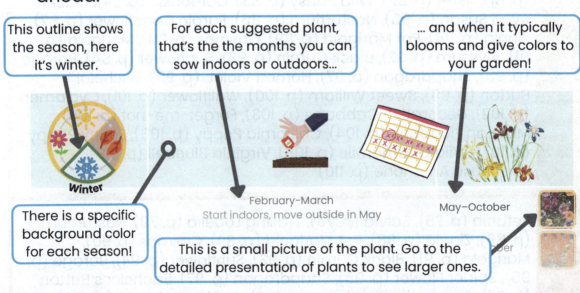

There is a specific background color for each season!

Winter

February–March
Start indoors, move outside in May

May–October

This is a small picture of the plant. Go to the detailed presentation of plants to see larger ones.

Ready to jump into the sowing and blooming breakdown?

Can You Find the Flower You Want to Plant this Season?

Most plants are sensitive to freezing temperatures. Why not start your plants indoors? This way, you can watch them sprout on a sunny windowsill. You may take them outdoors to provide color and happiness to your garden as the weather warms up, usually following the last spring frost.

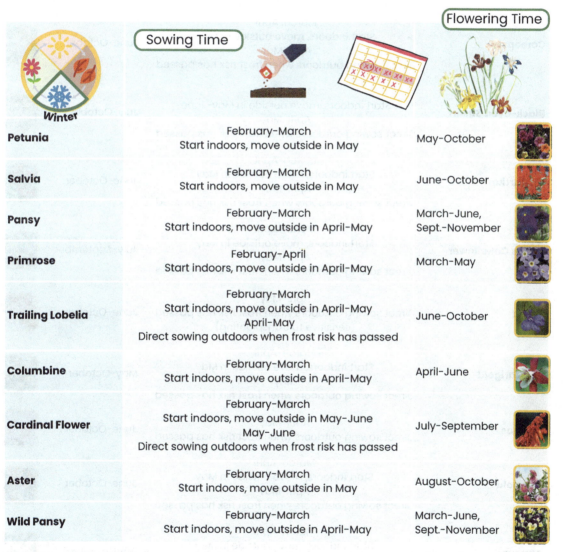

	Sowing Time	Flowering Time	
Petunia	February–March Start indoors, move outside in May	May–October	
Salvia	February–March Start indoors, move outside in May	June–October	
Pansy	February–March Start indoors, move outside in April–May	March–June, Sept.–November	
Primrose	February–April Start indoors, move outside in April–May	March–May	
Trailing Lobelia	February–March Start indoors, move outside in April–May April–May Direct sowing outdoors when frost risk has passed	June–October	
Columbine	February–March Start indoors, move outside in April–May	April–June	
Cardinal Flower	February–March Start indoors, move outside in May–June May–June Direct sowing outdoors when frost risk has passed	July–September	
Aster	February–March Start indoors, move outside in May	August–October	
Wild Pansy	February–March Start indoors, move outside in April–May	March–June, Sept.–November	

Excited to know more about these plants? Dive into their detailed profiles on pages with a light blue background!

Ready to find out which plants thrive in the warmer days of Spring?

Spring is the perfect time to get your hands dirty and start growing beautiful flowers! Some plants can be started indoors to protect them from frost, while others can go straight into the ground when it's warm. Can you find your favorites in this list? Get planting, and stay excited for the vibrant blooms of summer that come next!

Spring	Sowing Time		Flowering Time
Coreopsis	March–April Start indoors, move outside in May April–May Direct sowing outdoors when frost risk has passed		June–October
Black-eyed Susan	March–April Start indoors, move outside in May–June April–May Direct sowing outdoors when frost risk has passed		July–October
Nasturtium	March–April Start indoors, move outside in May April–May Direct sowing outdoors when frost risk has passed		June–October
Purple Coneflower	March–April Start indoors, move outside in May April–May Direct sowing outdoors when frost risk has passed		July–September
Zinnia	April–May Direct sowing outdoors when frost risk has passed (sensitive to transplanting)		June–October
Pot Marigold	March–April Start indoors, move outside in May May Direct sowing outdoors when frost risk has passed		May–October
Cosmos	April–May Direct sowing outdoors when frost risk has passed		June–October
Marigold	March–April Start indoors, move outside in May April–May Direct sowing outdoors when frost risk has passed		June–October
Alyssum	March–April Start indoors, move outside in May April–May Direct sowing outdoors when frost risk has passed		April–October
Black Cumin	March–April Direct sowing outdoors when frost risk has passed		May–July
Sunflower	April–May Direct sowing outdoors when frost risk has passed (sensitive to transplanting)		July–September

Summer is the perfect time to plant seeds and bulbs that will bring color to your garden in the months or even the following year! While some of these plants might bloom in just a few months, most of them are working hard to establish themselves for a vibrant display next year. Let's see which ones you can plant now to prepare for a colorful garden in the seasons to come!

	Sowing Time	Flowering Time
Borage	April-June Direct sowing outdoors when frost risk has passed	June-October
Spider Flower	May-June Direct sowing outdoors when frost risk has passed	July-October
Snapdragon	May-June Direct sowing outdoors when frost risk has passed	June-October
Horned Violet	May-June Direct sowing outdoors when frost risk has passed	April-October
Bachelor's Button	March-July Direct sowing outdoors when frost risk has passed	June-September
Sweet William	May-July for flowers the following spring (biennial)	May-July
Wallflower	June-July for flowers the following spring (biennial)	April-June
Cyclamen	July-August Plant **bulbs** indoors at cool temperatures (50–60°F) and move them outdoors when 50–60°F	October-December (outdoors)
Decorative Cabbage	July-August Direct sowing outdoors	September-Nov. (for foliage)
Mexican Fleabane	August-September Sowing outdoors for flowers next spring	April-October
Forget-me-not	August-September Sowing outdoors for flowers next spring (biennial)	April-June

Don't stop now! Fall brings its own set of colorful blooms. Flip the page to find out which flowers are perfect for planting as the leaves start to change.

Autumn may feel like the end of the growing season, but it's the perfect time to start planning for next year's blooms! Many plants need the cool temperatures of fall to prepare for a strong start in spring. By sowing these seeds now, you're giving them a head start for next year's garden. Let's see which flowers will thrive with a little fall planting!

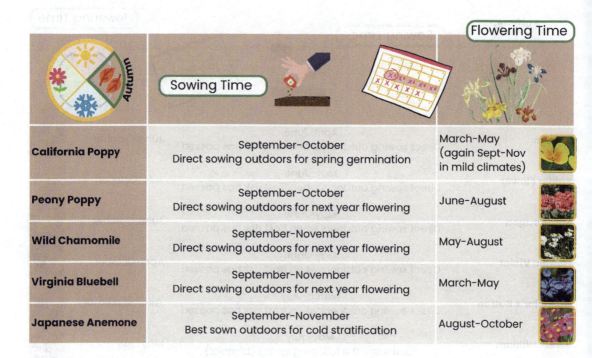

	Sowing Time	Flowering Time	
California Poppy	September–October Direct sowing outdoors for spring germination	March–May (again Sept–Nov in mild climates)	
Peony Poppy	September–October Direct sowing outdoors for next year flowering	June–August	
Wild Chamomile	September–November Direct sowing outdoors for next year flowering	May–August	
Virginia Bluebell	September–November Direct sowing outdoors for next year flowering	March–May	
Japanese Anemone	September–November Best sown outdoors for cold stratification	August–October	

With each season, your garden can offer something new! By planning your sowing and planting across the year, you'll enjoy a colorful display that lasts from spring through fall. So, keep an eye on the calendar and watch your garden bloom in every season!

Friendly Neighbor Flowers

Meet the Plants that Love to Grow Together!

Imagine your garden as a big neighborhood where different plants live next door to each other. Just like people, plants have their own personalities—and some make perfect neighbors! These "Friendly Neighbor" flowers help each other out, grow well side by side, or just look extra cool together.

What Are "Friendly Neighbor Flowers"?

Friendly Neighbor Flowers grow happily side by side. They don't compete for space, water, or sunlight—instead, they help each other and make the garden a beautiful, colorful place. Some Friendly Neighbors even attract butterflies and bees, which help the whole garden bloom and make it buzzing with life! Here's a peek at some of the most colorful, playful, and helpful Friendly Neighbors you can plant:

The Rainbow Team

| Salvia | Zinnia | Cosmos | Pot marigold | Marigold |

This is one of the brightest, boldest groups you can plant. These flowers come in every color from sunny yellow to fiery red, and they attract tons of butterflies and bees. Plus, they're super easy to grow, even if you're new to gardening! *What's your favorite Rainbow Team flower?*

Did you know? Marigolds can help keep certain garden pests away!

Want to Meet More Friendly Neighbors? The Rainbow Team is just the beginning! Flip the page to discover other flower friends.

Discover two other Friendly Neighbors!

The Magic Garden

Petunia

Trailing lobelia

Horned violet

Ever dreamed of a garden that looks like it belongs in a fairy tale? This team of purples, pinks, and blues brings magical colors to your garden. They're soft, lush, and love growing in shady spots.

Did you know? Petunias have a special scent that becomes stronger at night! This attracts night-flying pollinators like moths, which helps the flowers spread their seeds.

The Pollinator Party

Coreopsis

Black-eyed Susan

Aster

These flowers look like they're straight out of a wildflower meadow. They bloom in bright yellow and gold and are perfect for attracting pollinators like butterflies. Plus, they can handle some heat and don't need a lot of water, so they're low-maintenance, too!

Have you ever seen a butterfly visit a flower?

Did you know? Coreopsis flowers are sometimes called "tickseed" because their seeds look like tiny ticks! But don't worry, they're harmless and loved by birds.

Curious to Learn More About Each Friendly Neighbor?

Each Friendly Neighbor has a unique story! Explore 36 profiles to find fun facts, challenges, and tips—or mix and match them to create your own beautiful, buzzing garden!

Ready to Explore Flower's Unique Story?

Get ready, young gardener! You're about to dive into 36 amazing flower profiles that are as unique as you are. Each flower has its own special story, full of colors, fun facts, and challenges waiting for you to explore. From discovering where they grow best to seeing which ones attract butterflies, there's so much to learn and discover!

Here's What You'll Find

- **Water and Sun Needs ✹ 💧** — Each plant has its own needs for sunlight and water. Can you find the thirsty ones?
- **Bloom Times ◼** — Ever wonder when a flower is at its best? Check out the blooming months!
- **Special Flower Facts ✂** — What makes each flower unique? Discover hidden talents, like repelling pests or attracting pollinators.

How to Use This Guide

Flip through each page to discover the "personality" of every flower and start planning your dream garden! Look for the symbols to help you quickly understand what each plant needs. Ready to get started?

Let's go on this garden adventure and find the perfect flowers for your green space!

Symbols Used in Plant Presentations

Why don't you take a quick look at each plant presentation for the current period? Pay attention to the plant picture. Do you like it? If yes, compare your Hardiness Zone: can this plant thrive in your garden?

For example, if you live in Fairfax, VA, your zone is 7: can you tell if asters can thrive? Bingo! Aster can give colors to your garden!

Would they grow the same way if you lived in San Jose, CA? Try to find out!

This picture shows Asters of different colors. Do you like them?

Hardiness Zones Here it says aster do well in zones 4 to 8.

Waiting time before sprouting.

This icon shows the plant height at maturity.

This icon shows how easy or hard it is to grow this plant from seeds:
- Very difficult = 0 star
- Super easy = 5 stars

Aster
(Aster novae-angliae)

To Find Out More

Challenge

Which plants would match your garden? Check out their height and if they would thrive in your zone!

Symbols Used in Plant Presentations

Do you wonder how the plant will grow? Look at the timescale besides its picture!

In the aster example below, you'll learn that it's possible to sow the seeds indoors from February to March, and then transplant the plants outdoors in May, when temperatures are milder (60°F).

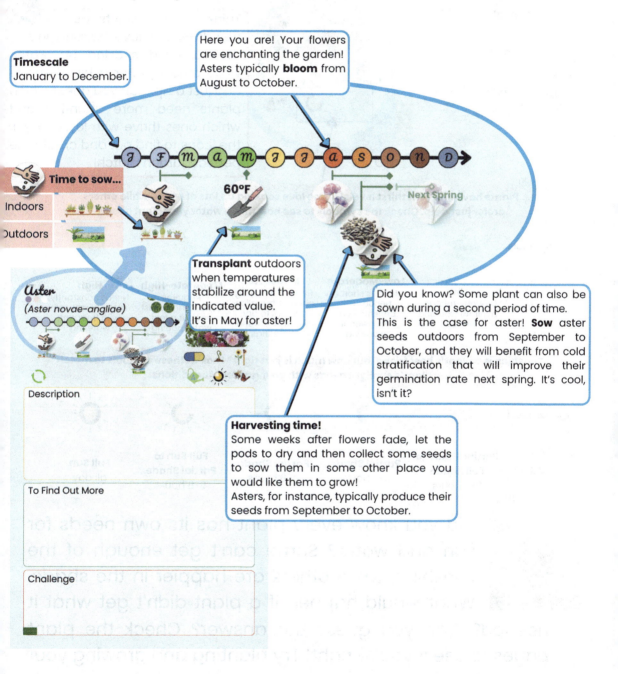

Timescale
January to December.

Here you are! Your flowers are enchanting the garden! Asters typically **bloom** from August to October.

Time to sow...

Indoors

Outdoors

60°F

Next Spring

Transplant outdoors when temperatures stabilize around the indicated value.
It's in May for aster!

Did you know? Some plant can also be sown during a second period of time.
This is the case for aster! **Sow** aster seeds outdoors from September to October, and they will benefit from cold stratification that will improve their germination rate next spring. It's cool, isn't it?

Harvesting time!
Some weeks after flowers fade, let the pods to dry and then collect some seeds to sow them in some other place you would like them to grow!
Asters, for instance, typically produce their seeds from September to October.

Aster
(Aster novae-angliae)

Description

To Find Out More

Challenge

What Does Your Plant Need to Thrive?

Every plant is unique! While all of them love sunlight and water, each one has its own special needs. Let's find out what they are and how to make them look healthy in your garden! Look at the icons just below the plant picture.

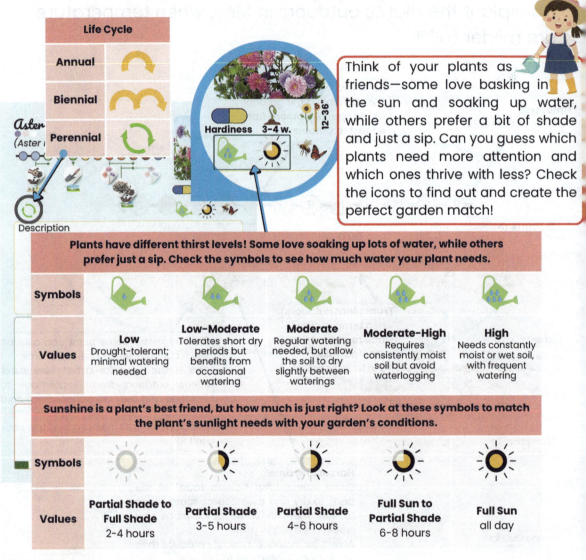

Think of your plants as friends—some love basking in the sun and soaking up water, while others prefer a bit of shade and just a sip. Can you guess which plants need more attention and which ones thrive with less? Check the icons to find out and create the perfect garden match!

Plants have different thirst levels! Some love soaking up lots of water, while others prefer just a sip. Check the symbols to see how much water your plant needs.

Symbols					
Values	**Low** Drought-tolerant; minimal watering needed	**Low-Moderate** Tolerates short dry periods but benefits from occasional watering	**Moderate** Regular watering needed, but allow the soil to dry slightly between waterings	**Moderate-High** Requires consistently moist soil but avoid waterlogging	**High** Needs constantly moist or wet soil, with frequent watering

Sunshine is a plant's best friend, but how much is just right? Look at these symbols to match the plant's sunlight needs with your garden's conditions.

Symbols					
Values	**Partial Shade to Full Shade** 2-4 hours	**Partial Shade** 3-5 hours	**Partial Shade** 4-6 hours	**Full Sun to Partial Shade** 6-8 hours	**Full Sun** all day

Did you know every plant has its own needs for sun and water? Some can't get enough of the sunshine, while others are happier in the shade. What would happen if a plant didn't get what it needed? Can you guess the answer? Check the plant pages to see if you're right! Try planting and growing your flowers in different parts of your garden with varying sun exposure to discover their favorite spots.

Meet Your Plant Friends and Visitors!

Discover how plants use their colors and scents to attract visitors like hummingbirds, butterflies and bees! Do you know why plants have scientific names? It's to capture their varieties and unique identity! For example, there are around 200 types of asters! Botanists use special scientific names to identify and track all these varieties. These names help identify each unique type, just like a first and last name for plants!

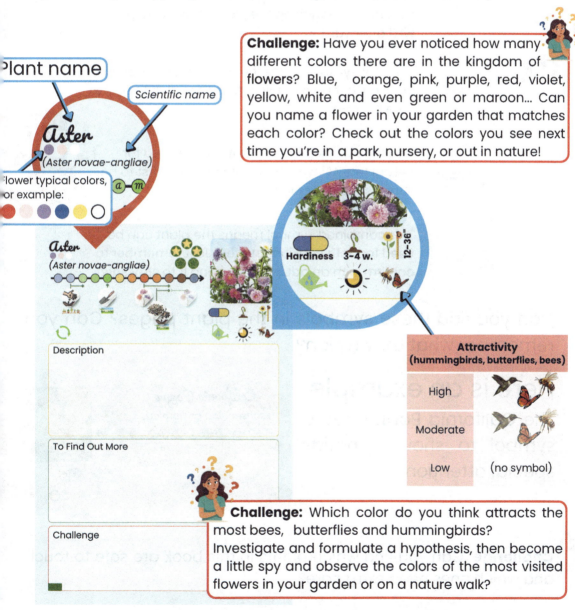

Plant name

Scientific name

Aster

(Aster novae-angliae)

Flower typical colors, for example:

Challenge: Have you ever noticed how many different colors there are in the kingdom of flowers? Blue, orange, pink, purple, red, violet, yellow, white and even green or maroon... Can you name a flower in your garden that matches each color? Check out the colors you see next time you're in a park, nursery, or out in nature!

Aster
(Aster novae-angliae)

Hardiness 3–4 w. 12–36"

Attractivity
(hummingbirds, butterflies, bees)

High	
Moderate	
Low	(no symbol)

Description

To Find Out More

Challenge

Challenge: Which color do you think attracts the most bees, butterflies and hummingbirds? Investigate and formulate a hypothesis, then become a little spy and observe the colors of the most visited flowers in your garden or on a nature walk?

Explore your garden and note how many types of visitors you can spot!

Special Plant Properties

Did you know that some plants can be both fun and tricky? Let's discover what their symbols mean so you know how to handle them safely!

Symbol	Meaning
⚠ TOXIC	**Be careful!** This symbol means the plant is toxic. Always wear gloves when touching it, like the leaves or seeds. Never put your hands near your mouth after touching the plant. Wash your hands well afterward.
🌿	This leaf symbol shows the plant can be used in cooking. But before trying it, ask an adult to make sure it's safe.
☕	This teacup means the plant can be used for herbal tea. Always check with an adult first to be sure it's the right plant!
☕🍴	This combined symbol means the plant can be used for both cooking and tea. Just remember to confirm with an adult before using it to stay safe!

Can you find these symbols in the plant pages? Can you remember what they mean?

Here is an example

The California Poppy has a symbol to show it needs special attention.

Challenge: Can you find which plants in this book are safe to touch and which ones need extra care?

You're ready to be a garden detective! Go on, explore the plants and find all the symbols!

Petunia

Petunia × atkinsiana)

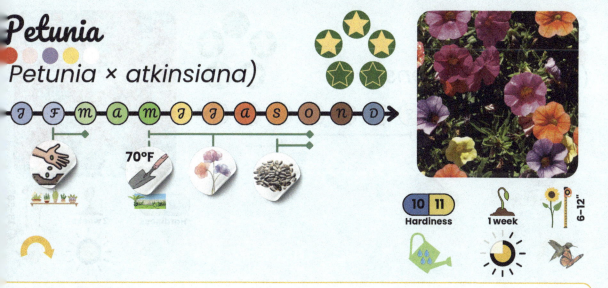

J F M A M J J A S O N D

70°F

10 11 Hardiness

1 week

6–12"

Description

Petunias are colorful, trumpet-shaped flowers that bloom in bright shades of pink, purple, red, and white. These flowers love the sun and bloom all summer long, making them perfect for hanging baskets, pots, or garden beds. Petunias need regular watering to stay happy, especially in hot weather. They're great for adding lots of color to your garden or patio!

To Find Out More

Petunia × atkinsiana is a hybrid flower that's been cultivated to combine beauty and resilience. Petunias were first discovered in South America and have become one of the most popular garden flowers in the world. They come in a wide variety of colors and patterns, including striped and speckled flowers. Petunias are also known for their ability to repel certain garden pests, making them useful as companion plants. Plus, their sweet fragrance is a bonus in any garden!

Challenge

Experiment with growing petunias in different containers! Try planting them in hanging baskets, pots, or directly in the garden. Track which method helps them bloom the most. You can also try mixing colors to create a rainbow petunia garden. Keep a journal of your watering schedule and note how it affects the flowers' growth.

Salvia
(Salvia splendens)

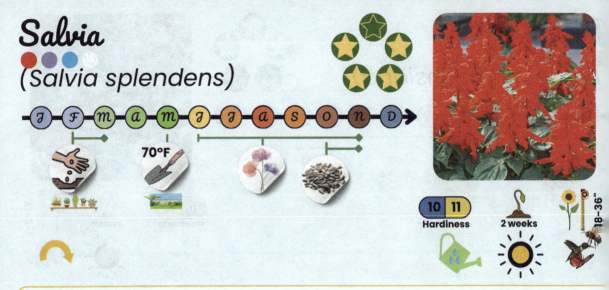

J F M A M J J A S O N D

70°F

10 | 11
Hardiness

2 weeks

18-36"

Description

Salvia splendens, commonly known as scarlet sage, gets its name from the vibrant, fiery red flowers that bloom in tall spikes. These flowers are a favorite of hummingbirds and butterflies, and they thrive in full sun. Blooming all summer and into fall, scarlet sage is easy to grow and perfect for garden beds or borders. Its bold color and height make it especially stunning when planted in groups, creating a vivid display in any garden.

To Find Out More

Salvia splendens, also known as scarlet sage, is native to Brazil and has become a popular garden flower around the world. It's a favorite for attracting pollinators like hummingbirds, thanks to its vibrant red color. In addition to being beautiful, salvia plants are part of the mint family and have been used in herbal medicine for centuries. Some varieties of Salvia are even used to make teas and spices, although *Salvia splendens* is mostly grown for its striking blooms.

Challenge

Attract hummingbirds to your garden with scarlet sage! Plant the flowers in a sunny spot and keep track of how often the hummingbirds visit. You can also experiment with planting different colors of salvia and note which ones attract the most pollinators. Draw or photograph the hummingbirds that visit and write about your experience!

Pansy
(Viola)

Description

Violas, or pansies, are small but colorful flowers that come in shades of purple, yellow, blue, and more. These flowers have a cute "face" in the center, making them easy to recognize! They grow in cool weather and are often seen in spring and fall gardens. Violas love sunny spots but can handle some shade too. Their flowers are edible, so you can even use them to decorate cakes and salads!

To Find Out More

Violas are known as symbols of thoughtfulness. In fact, the name "pansy" comes from the French word "pensée", meaning "thought." While they look delicate, Violas are hardy plants that can withstand light frosts. They're also one of the few flowers that can bloom in winter if the weather isn't too harsh. In medieval times, people believed that Violas could bring love and luck!

Challenge

Design your edible flower garden! Grow *Violas* alongside other edible flowers like nasturtiums. Use them to decorate cupcakes or make colorful salads. Keep track of how well each type grows and which one blooms first. Don't forget to take pictures and create a flower recipe book!
Care for your pansies during the warmer summer time, and you'll enjoy seeing them blooming again in autumn!

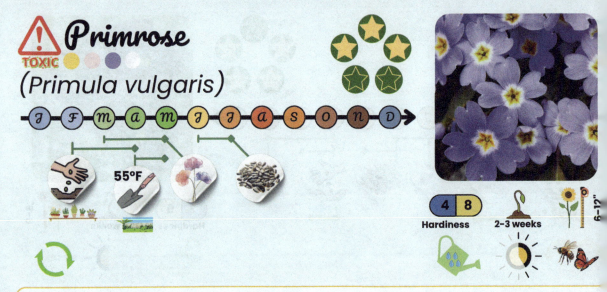

Primrose
TOXIC
(Primula vulgaris)

J F m a m J J a s o n D

55°F

4 | 8
Hardiness

2-3 weeks

6-12"

Description

Primroses are early bloomers that love cooler weather. Their flowers come in a rainbow of colors like yellow, pink, purple, and white. They grow close to the ground, with pretty leaves surrounding their blooms. Primroses like shady areas and lots of water, making them perfect for gardens in spring. They attract butterflies and other pollinators, which makes them a fun plant to watch!

To Find Out More

Primroses are one of the first flowers to bloom in spring, earning them their name, which means "first rose." They're not just pretty—they've been used in traditional medicine for centuries. Early settlers used Primrose leaves in teas to soothe coughs and colds. The flowers are also an important food source for early pollinators like bees and butterflies when not much else is blooming!

Challenge

Create a butterfly garden with primroses! Keep track of which pollinators visit your flowers—are they bees, butterflies, or something else? Try planting them in different parts of your garden to see where they grow best. Which location attracts the most butterflies? Record your findings and draw pictures of the pollinators you spot.

Safety Note: Primroses are generally safe, but some species may cause mild skin irritation or allergic reactions in sensitive individuals. Always wash your hands after handling the plant and avoid touching your face to prevent irritation. If irritation occurs, rinse thoroughly with water.

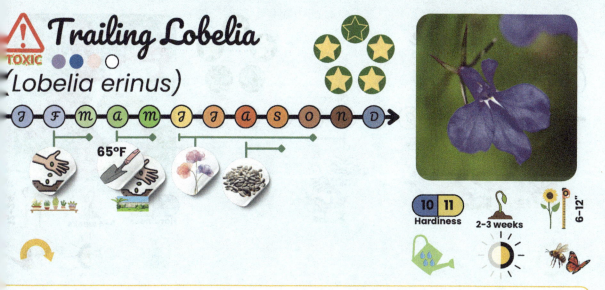

TOXIC Trailing Lobelia
(Lobelia erinus)

65°F

10 | 11
Hardiness

2-3 weeks

6-12"

Description

Trailing lobelia is a colorful plant with flowers in shades of blue, purple, pink, and white. It's great for adding pops of color to gardens and hanging baskets. Trailing lobelia loves sunny spots but can also grow in some shade. It's a low-growing plant, so it looks like a blanket of tiny flowers! Trailing lobelia blooms all summer long, making it a favorite for gardeners who want their gardens to stay bright.

To Find Out More

Lobelia erinus is native to Southern Africa, where it thrives in warm weather. Interestingly, the flower's petals are often two-toned, with a darker shade on the lower petals and a lighter color on the top. *Lobelia erinus* is named after the botanist Matthias de L'Obel, who studied plants in the 16th century. While Lobelia erinus isn't the biggest pollinator magnet, its bright colors still attract bees and butterflies throughout summer.

Challenge

Create a hanging garden with *Lobelia erinus*! Plant *Lobelia erinus* in a basket and hang it in a sunny spot. Track how quickly the flowers grow and see how long the blooms last. Try experimenting with different watering schedules to see how it affects the plant. Does the *Lobelia erinus* bloom more when watered regularly, or can it handle dry spells?
Safety Note: *Lobelia erinus* can be a bit tricky—it's safe to touch, but don't let anyone eat it! Always wash your hands after handling the plant, and keep an eye on younger siblings or friends to make sure they don't put any part of it in their mouths.

⚠ Columbine
TOXIC
(Aquilegia)

3 | 9 Hardiness

3-4 weeks

12-24"

Description
Columbine is a beautiful plant with unique, star-shaped flowers that come in colors like red, pink, purple, yellow, and blue. It has long, graceful stems and loves to grow in gardens that get some shade. Hummingbirds, bees, and butterflies love columbine because of its sweet nectar. The flowers bloom in late spring and early summer, making them a great addition to any garden!

To Find Out More
Columbine has an interesting history! In medieval times, it was known as a symbol of courage and love. The plant has evolved a special shape to attract hummingbirds, with long, tube-like flowers perfectly designed for their long beaks. Columbine is also known for its resilience—it can grow in many different environments, from shady gardens to open meadows. In some cultures, it's considered a lucky flower!

Challenge
Attract hummingbirds to your garden with columbines! Plant them in a spot that gets partial shade and keep a lookout for these tiny birds. Try sitting quietly near the flowers to observe the hummingbirds as they visit. Write down the times they come and how many you spot. If you're lucky, you might even see them sipping nectar!

Safety Note: Did you know columbine seeds and roots can be harmful if eaten? Make sure to wash your hands after planting or caring for them. If you're gardening with little ones, help them stay safe by reminding them not to pick or play with the seeds or roots.

Cardinal Flower
Lobelia cardinalis)

TOXIC

65°F

3 | 9
Hardiness

3-4 weeks

24-36"

Description

The cardinal flower is a striking plant with bright red flowers that grow on tall stems. It gets its name from its vivid red color, similar to a cardinal's feathers. This flower loves wet areas, so it's perfect for planting near ponds or streams. The cardinal flower blooms in late summer and is a favorite for hummingbirds looking for nectar!

To Find Out More

Cardinal flowers are named after the red robes worn by Catholic cardinals. Native to North America, these flowers have adapted to thrive in moist environments, making them great for water gardens. Interestingly, their bright red color is rare among flowers and is highly attractive to hummingbirds, who are one of the few creatures able to see red clearly. The cardinal flower has also been used in traditional medicine by Native Americans for its healing properties.

Challenge

Plant a water garden with cardinal flowers! Find a spot in your garden that stays moist or create a small pond area. Track how well the cardinal flowers grow in different spots. Do they bloom better near water? Observe the hummingbirds that visit, and try to capture their visits with photos or drawings. Keep a journal of what you see!

Safety Note: Cardinal flowers contain compounds that can be mildly toxic if ingested. Avoid licking or putting your fingers near your mouth after handling the plant. Always wash your hands thoroughly afterward. Use gloves if handling leaves, stems, or flowers for extended periods, and keep the plant out of reach of pets and small children.

Aster

(Aster novae-angliae)

4	8
Hardiness	

3-4 weeks

12-36"

Description

New England asters are tall, beautiful flowers with purple, pink, or white petals and bright yellow centers. They bloom in late summer and fall, bringing lots of color to the garden when other flowers are fading. Asters love the sun and attract butterflies and bees, making them perfect for pollinator-friendly gardens!

To Find Out More

Aster novae-angliae, or New England aster, is a native plant of North America and is a key flower for late-season pollinators. As one of the last flowers to bloom before winter, asters provide an important food source for butterflies and bees. The name "aster" comes from the Greek word for "star," reflecting the shape of the flower's petals. New England asters are also known for their ability to tolerate cold, and they can even handle light frosts!

Challenge

Create a butterfly haven with New England asters! Plant them in a sunny spot and track how many butterflies visit the flowers in the fall. Keep a journal to record the different types of butterflies and their favorite times to visit. You can also try collecting seeds from the flowers and planting them next year!

Wild Pansy
Viola tricolor)

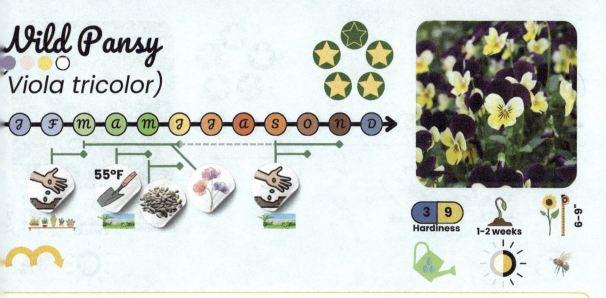

J F m a m J J a s o n D

55°F

3 9
Hardiness

1-2 weeks

6-9"

Description

Viola tricolor, also known as Johnny jump-up and wild pansy, gets its names for two reasons. "Johnny jump-up" refers to its ability to "jump up" quickly in gardens, often appearing unexpectedly. "Wild pansy" comes from it being the wild ancestor of garden pansies. This small flower has vibrant purple, yellow, and white petals, and it thrives in cool weather and loves both sun and shade. It's easy to grow and edible—its colorful petals are perfect for decorating cakes or adding to salads.

To Find Out More

Viola tricolor, or wild pansy, has been used in traditional herbal medicine for centuries, especially in Europe. It was believed to have healing properties for skin conditions and respiratory problems. The name "Johnny jump-up" comes from how quickly and easily these flowers appear in gardens, often growing from seeds that were scattered by the wind. Besides being pretty, their petals are edible, adding a sweet, mild flavor to food.

Challenge

Create your own edible flower garden with Johnny jump-ups! Try using the flowers as garnishes on cupcakes or in salads. Track how quickly the flowers bloom and which areas of your garden they grow best in—sunny spots or shady ones? Keep a recipe book of creative ways to use these edible flowers!

Coreopsis
(Coreopsis)

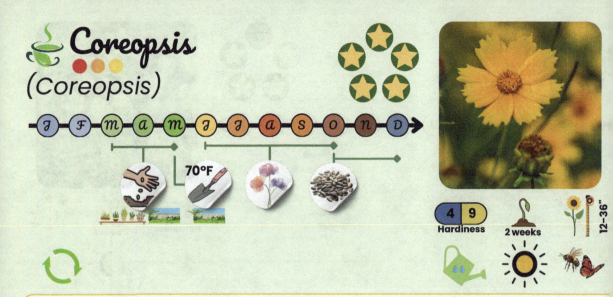

J F m a m J J a S O n D

70°F

4 9 Hardiness

2 weeks

12–36"

Description

Coreopsis, also known as tickseed, is a sunny flower that blooms in shades of yellow, orange, and red. These flowers love the sun and can handle dry weather, making them great for summer gardens. Coreopsis blooms for a long time and attracts bees and butterflies. They're easy to grow and perfect for adding bright colors to your garden!

To Find Out More

Coreopsis is a native wildflower in North America and is known for its ability to thrive in poor soil. Its name comes from the Greek word "koris", meaning bug, because its seeds resemble small ticks. *Coreopsis* is a favorite for wildflower gardens because it attracts pollinators like bees, butterflies, and hoverflies. The flowers can also be used to make a mild tea, and some species of *Coreopsis* have been used in traditional herbal medicine.

Challenge

Plant a pollinator-friendly garden with *Coreopsis*! See how many bees and butterflies visit your flowers and track their activity throughout the summer. You can also experiment with making tea from the dried flowers. Keep a garden journal where you record which pollinators visit the most and how well the plants grow in different spots.

Black-Eyed Susan
Rudbeckia hirta)

J F m a m J J a s o n D

70°F

3 9
Hardiness   1-3 weeks   24-36"

Description
Black-eyed Susan is a bright and cheerful flower with yellow petals and a dark brown center. It grows tall and blooms in the summer and fall, attracting butterflies and bees. Black-eyed Susans love sunny spots and can handle dry weather once they're grown. These flowers are easy to grow and make gardens look sunny and happy all season long!

To Find Out More
Rudbeckia hirta is a native plant to North America and is often used to restore prairies and meadows. They are known for their resilience—they can handle poor soil and dry conditions. The flower is named after Olof Rudbeck, a Swedish botanist, and its dark center resembles an eye, which is how it got the name "Black-eyed." These flowers are important for pollinators and help support the ecosystem by providing food for bees and butterflies.

Challenge
Create a pollinator paradise! Plant black-eyed Susans alongside other pollinator-friendly flowers like coneflowers and zinnias. Keep track of how many butterflies and bees visit your flowers each day. Can you spot the differences between the types of pollinators? Try sketching them and note which flowers attract the most!

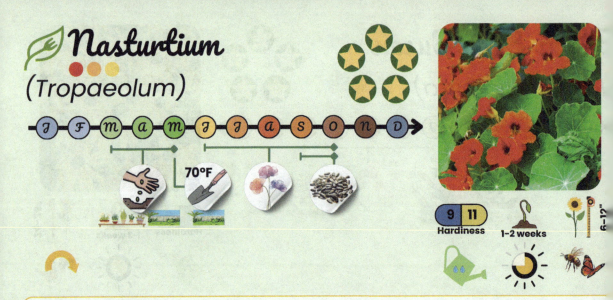

Nasturtium
(Tropaeolum)

J F m a m J J a s o n D

70°F

9 | 11
Hardiness

1-2 weeks

6-12"

Description

Nasturtiums are fun, colorful flowers that grow quickly and are easy to care for. They bloom in bright shades of red, orange, and yellow, adding lots of color to any garden. Nasturtiums are also special because you can eat their flowers and leaves! They have a peppery taste that's perfect for salads. These flowers love the sun and don't mind if the soil gets a little dry.

To Find Out More

Tropaeolums are not only pretty but also practical! They are known as "companion plants" because they help protect other plants from pests like aphids. Their leaves and flowers are edible, with a peppery flavor similar to watercress. In the past, people used *Tropaeolum* leaves to treat colds due to their high vitamin C content. Another cool fact? *Tropaeolums* are popular among pollinators, especially bees and hummingbirds, making them great for your garden's health!

Challenge

Try planting *Tropaeolums* around your vegetable garden as natural pest control! Keep a journal of how well they grow and which pests they repel. You can also try harvesting the leaves and flowers to create your own peppery salad or pickling the seeds as a caper substitute. Don't forget to taste and share your results!

Purple Coneflower
Echinacea purpurea)

J - F - m - a - m - J - J - a - s - o - n - D

70°F

3 9 Hardiness 1-3 weeks 24-36"

Description
Purple coneflowers are tall, bright flowers with purple petals and spiky, orange centers. They bloom in the summer and are loved by bees, butterflies, and even birds! Purple coneflowers are tough plants that can grow in dry soil and full sun. They are also used in herbal medicine, making them both pretty and useful in the garden.

To Find Out More
Echinacea purpurea, or purple coneflower, is famous for its medicinal uses. The roots and leaves are often used to make herbal teas and supplements to help boost the immune system and fight off colds. These flowers are also excellent for wildlife gardens—they attract pollinators in summer and provide seeds for birds like goldfinches in the fall. Plus, *Echinacea* is drought-tolerant, making it a perfect plant for hot, dry summers.

Challenge
Create your own nature study with *Echinacea*! Track how many pollinators visit your flowers each day—do you see more bees or butterflies? In the fall, leave the seed heads on the plant and watch for birds that come to eat the seeds. Keep a journal of your observations and take pictures or draw what you see.

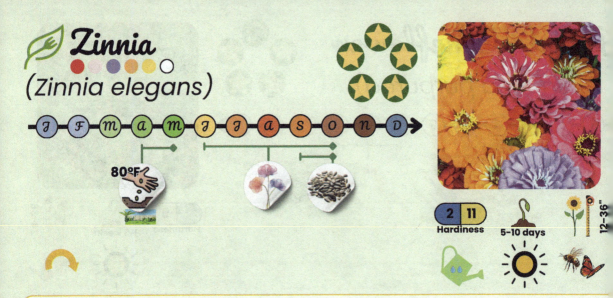

Zinnia
(Zinnia elegans)

2 | 11 Hardiness

5-10 days

12-36"

Description

Zinnias are colorful, cheerful flowers that bloom in bright shades like pink, purple, yellow, and red. They love the sun and grow quickly, making them perfect for summer gardens. Zinnias bloom all season long, attracting butterflies and bees to your garden. These flowers are easy to grow and add a splash of color that lasts for months!

To Find Out More

Zinnias are native to Mexico and have been grown for centuries for their bright colors and long-lasting blooms. Did you know that zinnias can help your garden stay healthy? They attract pollinators like butterflies and bees, which help other plants grow. Zinnias are also drought-tolerant, meaning they can handle dry weather once they're established. Plus, their flowers are long-lasting in bouquets, making them popular with gardeners who like to bring flowers indoors!

Challenge

Create a butterfly garden with zinnias! Plant different colors and observe which butterflies visit the most. Keep a butterfly diary, noting the different types and how often they come. You can also experiment with cutting zinnias for bouquets—how long do the flowers last indoors compared to in the garden? Record your findings!

Pot Marigold
Calendula officinalis)

Description

Calendula officinalis, also called pot marigold, is a bright yellow or orange flower that blooms for a long time—from spring all the way to fall. It's a super easy plant to grow and doesn't need much care. *Calendula* petals are edible and can be used to decorate cakes or salads. These flowers love the sun and are great for brightening up any garden!

To Find Out More

Calendula has been used for centuries as a healing plant. In ancient times, its petals were used in medicines to treat cuts and skin problems. Today, it's often added to lotions and creams because of its soothing properties. *Calendula* is also sometimes called "poor man's saffron" because its petals can be used to color and flavor food like rice or soups. Plus, this flower attracts beneficial insects like bees and hoverflies that help your garden thrive.

Challenge

Create your own *Calendula* skin balm! Harvest *Calendula* petals, dry them, and mix them with oil to make a soothing skin lotion. You can also try using the petals to color rice or bake them into cookies as a fun experiment. Keep track of your results and share your creations with family or friends!

Cosmos
(Cosmos bipinnatus)

J F m a m J J a s o n D

70°F

2 | 11
Hardiness

5-10 days

24-60"

Description

Cosmos are tall, beautiful flowers that bloom in summer and fall. They come in bright colors like pink, white, and purple, and they love the sun. Cosmos are super easy to grow and don't need a lot of water, which makes them perfect for beginner gardeners. They bloom all summer long and attract butterflies and bees to the garden.

To Find Out More

Cosmos bipinnatus flowers are native to Mexico, where they grow in dry, sunny areas. They are famous for their ability to thrive in poor soil and don't need much water, which is why they're called "drought-tolerant." *Cosmos bipinnatus* are also loved by pollinators like bees and butterflies. Their name comes from the Greek word "kosmos", meaning "harmony" or "order," because of the flower's balanced petals.

Challenge

Try growing *Cosmos bipinnatus* in different spots in your garden! Plant some in full sun and others in partial shade. Which ones grow taller or bloom more? Track your results by measuring the height of the plants and the number of flowers they produce. You can also collect seeds from the flowers at the end of the season and try growing them again next year!

Marigold
(Tagetes)

J F M A M J J A S O N D

70°F

2 | 11
Hardiness

5-7 days

6-24"

Description
Marigolds are bright, cheerful flowers that bloom in shades of yellow, orange, and red. They grow quickly and love sunny gardens, making them perfect for beginner gardeners. Marigolds are not only pretty but also helpful—they can keep pests away from other plants in your garden. They bloom all summer long, adding lots of color to your outdoor spaces!

To Find Out More
Tagetes have been grown for thousands of years, and ancient civilizations like the Aztecs used them in ceremonies and medicines. Their petals can be used in cooking to add color and a spicy, citrusy flavor to salads and soups. One of their coolest tricks is their ability to repel pests like aphids, which makes them great companion plants for vegetable gardens. *Tagetes* are also used in festivals like Día de los Muertos in Mexico, where they symbolize remembrance.

Challenge
Try creating a natural pest-repellent garden with *Tagetes*! Plant them around your vegetables or other flowers and track how well they keep pests away. Record which insects you see near your plants. You can also harvest *Tagetes* petals to dry and use in cooking—try adding them to a salad and see how they taste!

Alyssum
(Lobularia maritima)

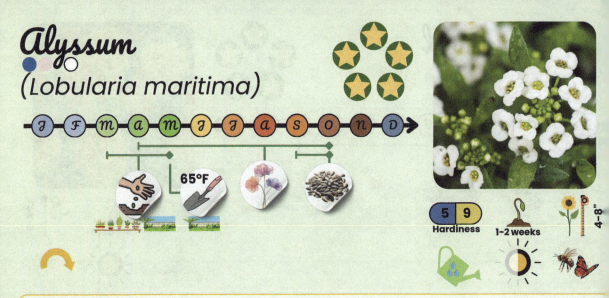

J F m a m J J a s o n D

65°F

5 9 Hardiness   1-2 weeks   4-8"

Description

Alyssum is a low-growing plant with tiny flowers that bloom in white, pink, or purple. These flowers are also called sweet alyssum because they have a sweet, honey-like scent. They are perfect for filling in garden borders or hanging baskets. Alyssum blooms in spring and fall, and it loves sunny spots. This plant is super easy to grow and adds a delicate touch to any garden!

To Find Out More

Alyssum is native to the Mediterranean and is well-loved for its sweet fragrance. The plant is great for attracting beneficial insects like hoverflies, which help control pests in your garden. Alyssum is also popular in rock gardens or as a ground cover because it grows close to the ground and spreads quickly. The flowers can even tolerate light frosts, making them a good choice for cooler weather gardens.

Challenge

Create a sweet-smelling garden with alyssum! Plant it along garden borders or in hanging baskets and note how fast it spreads. See if you can detect the honey-like scent on warm days and track which insects visit the flowers. Try planting it in both sunny and shady spots to observe how the plant grows differently. Record your observations in a garden journal.

Black Cumin
Nigella sativa)

J F m a m J J a s o n D

65°F

2 11 Hardiness

1–2 weeks

12–18"

Description
Black cumin is a small, delicate plant with pretty white or pale blue flowers. It grows best in sunny spots and doesn't need much water, making it easy to care for. The seeds, called black cumin or black seed, are famous for their use in cooking. The plant grows quickly from seeds, so it's a great choice for young gardeners who want to see results fast!

To Find Out More
Did you know that black cumin seeds have been used for over 2,000 years? Ancient Egyptians even found black cumin seeds in King Tutankhamun's tomb! The seeds are packed with nutrients and are used in dishes around the world for their slightly spicy flavor. The plant is tough, growing well in dry and sunny places, which helps it survive in places with little rain.

Challenge
Plant some black cumin seeds and keep track of their growth. How long do they take to sprout? Once they bloom, try collecting the seeds. Research how black cumin seeds are used in different recipes. Can you create your own simple dish using the seeds? You could even try drying and grinding them to see how their flavor changes!

Sunflower
(Helianthus annuus)

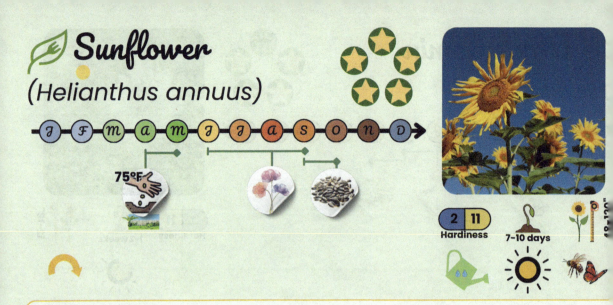

Hardiness 2 11

7–10 days

Description
Sunflowers are tall, bright flowers with yellow petals and a dark center. They love the sun so much that they follow it all day, turning their heads to soak up every bit of sunlight! Sunflowers can grow as tall as you or even taller. Not only are they fun to watch, but their seeds are also tasty snacks for people, birds, and squirrels!

To Find Out More
Sunflowers are native to North America and have been used by Native Americans for food, oil, and medicine for thousands of years. These amazing plants can grow up to 12 feet tall and are known for their ability to track the sun—a behavior called **heliotropism**. Sunflower seeds are packed with nutrients and are a popular snack, both roasted and raw. Even the flower buds are edible and can be cooked like artichokes! Sunflowers are also great for attracting pollinators and birds to your garden.

Challenge
Grow your own giant sunflowers! Measure how tall it gets and track how it follows the sun each day. But does this behavior continue forever? Why? Observe and find out! You can also harvest the seeds to eat or share with the birds. Try roasting them and compare the taste to raw seeds. Keep a growth journal and take pictures to document the process!

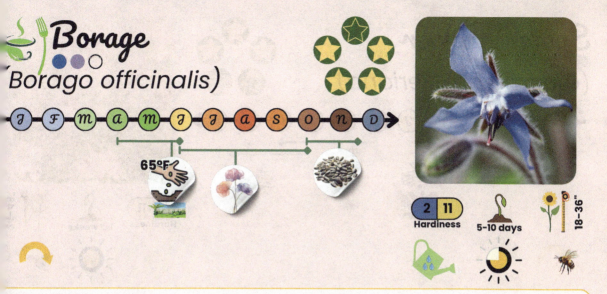

Borage
(*Borago officinalis*)

J F M A M J J A S O N D

65°F

2 | 11
Hardiness

5-10 days

18-36"

Description
Borage is a fascinating plant with star-shaped, bright blue flowers and fuzzy stems! Its flowers look a bit like stars and add a beautiful pop of color to any garden. Borage grows well in sunny spots and doesn't mind a bit of poor soil. Besides being pretty, it's known for attracting friendly pollinators like bees and butterflies. Did you know that borage leaves and flowers are even edible? They add a fresh, cucumber-like taste to salads!

To Find Out More
Did you know borage has a special connection with bees? Its blue flowers produce nectar so abundantly that it's a favorite among bees! This plant has been used in gardens for centuries, not only for its beauty but also for its healing properties—some cultures even called it the "herb of gladness." Another unique trait is that borage flowers can turn pink as they age, creating a blend of blue and pink stars in your garden. What a colorful transformation!

Challenge
Create a "Bee-Watch" diary! Plant borage in your garden, then observe how many bees visit each day. Try counting at different times to see when bees prefer to visit. As a bonus challenge, see if you can find borage flowers that have changed color. Keep track of your findings, and use your diary to see if your borage plants attract more pollinators over time. You could even draw the changes you see in the garden!

Spider Flower
(Cleome hassleriana)

75°F

10 11 Hardiness

1-2 weeks

24-48"

Description

Spider flowers are unique, tall plants with long, spindly petals that look a bit like spider legs! Kids can plant them from June to September for an impressive, late-summer bloom. These flowers come in shades of pink, purple, and white, and they grow best in sunny spots with well-drained soil. spider flowers can reach up to 4 feet tall, making them a standout in the garden. Plus, they're great at attracting butterflies and hummingbirds!

To Find Out More

Spider flowers have an interesting trick up their "sleeves"! They can grow quickly in summer, even in less-than-perfect soil, which makes them perfect for tough spots in the garden. Their tall stalks and distinctive flowers attract pollinators like hummingbirds and butterflies. In some places, spider flowers have even been used as a natural insect repellent! This plant's adaptability and unique structure make it a fascinating addition to any garden.

Challenge

Create a "Pollinator Journal"! After planting your spider flowers, keep a record of all the pollinators you spot visiting them. Note the time of day and type of pollinator, like bees, butterflies, or hummingbirds. Do you see different visitors on sunny days versus cloudy ones? Try sketching your spider flowers and their visitors. At the end of the season, see which pollinator was the most common visitor!

Snapdragon
(Antirrhinum majus)

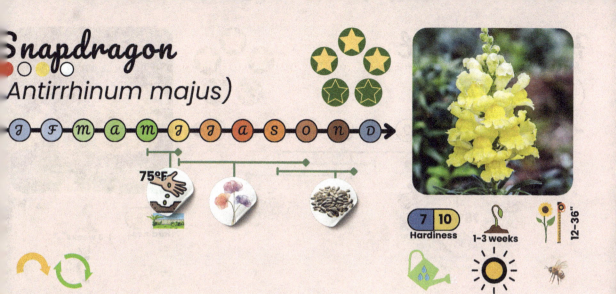

J F m a m J J a s o n D

75°F

7 10 Hardiness · 1-3 weeks · 12-36"

Description

Snapdragons are fun, colorful flowers that look like tiny dragon mouths! Plant them from June to September, and they'll bloom in bright shades of pink, red, yellow, and more. Snapdragons grow best in sunny spots, and they make great companions for other flowers. Kids love giving these flowers a gentle squeeze to see the "dragon" open its mouth. Snapdragons are also excellent for attracting pollinators to the garden.

To Find Out More

Snapdragons have a fascinating biology! Their "dragon mouth" shape evolved to attract certain types of pollinators, especially bumblebees. Only strong insects can open the "jaws" to reach the nectar inside! In the past, snapdragons were thought to ward off evil, and they were even used in old-fashioned remedies. Their scientific name, *Antirrhinum*, means "like a nose" in Greek—quite fitting for a flower with such a unique shape!

Challenge

Try a "Snapdragon Pollinator Test"! Once your snapdragons bloom, observe which insects can open the "dragon's mouth" to reach the nectar. Do smaller insects struggle, while larger ones like bumblebees have no trouble? Record your findings in a journal, noting how the flowers react to different pollinators. You could even design a simple experiment to test which pollinators prefer Snapdragons the most!

Horned Violet
(Viola cornuta)

Description

Horned violets, also known as tufted pansies, are small, cheerful flowers that bloom in shades of purple, yellow, and blue. Kids can plant them from June through September to add a splash of color in the garden or pots. These flowers enjoy a bit of shade, so they're perfect for spots that don't get full sun. Their petals are soft and velvety, making them a favorite among gardeners and flower lovers alike!

To Find Out More

Horned violets have a curious name! They're called "horned" because of the small spur, or "horn," that extends from the back of the flower. These flowers have a long history as symbols of love and thoughtfulness. Some people believe they can bring luck to gardens! They're also quite resilient, often blooming in cooler weather when other flowers start to fade.

Challenge

Create a "Shade Garden Experiment"! Plant horned violets in different shaded spots around the garden—under trees, near walls, or beside taller plants. Keep a journal to track how well they grow in each location. Which spot has the most flowers? Do the violets prefer more or less shade? At the end of the season, you'll discover the best place for Horned Violets in your garden!

Bachelor's Button

● ○ ○

(Centaurea cyanus)

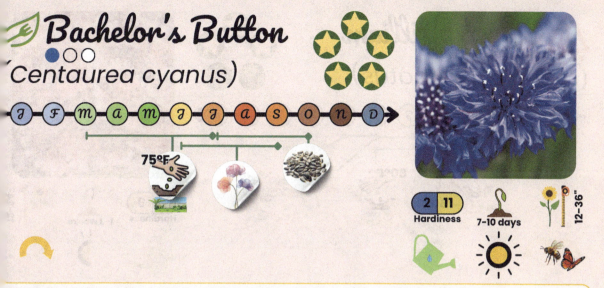

J F M A M J J A S O N D

75°F

2 11 Hardiness

7-10 days

12-36"

Description

Bachelor's button, or cornflower, is a bright blue flower that looks a bit like a small, spiky star. You can plant them in the garden from June to September for a pop of color. They love full sun and can handle dry soil, so they're easy to care for. Plus, bachelor's button is great for making wildflower bouquets, as they're long-lasting and bring a touch of blue to any arrangement.

To Find Out More

Bachelor's button has a rich history as a symbol of love and luck. In ancient times, young men would wear these flowers to show their affection, giving it the name "bachelor's button." This flower is also known for its resilience and can grow in areas where other plants struggle. Its blue pigment, called protocyanin, is rare in nature, making bachelor's button a unique find in the garden.

Challenge

Make a "Wildflower Bouquet"! Once your bachelor's buttons bloom, pick a few and mix them with other flowers in your garden to create a colorful arrangement. Try drying some bachelor's buttons by hanging them upside down in a dark spot—they keep their color well! Compare fresh and dried flowers, and see how long each lasts. This way, you can enjoy your garden flowers all year long!

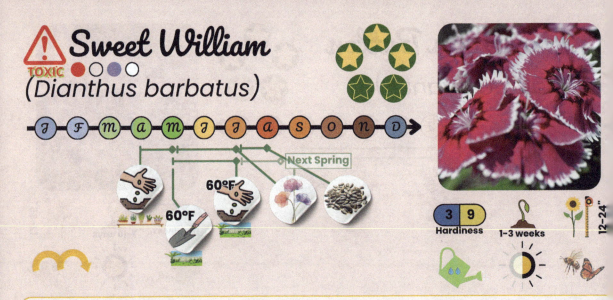

Sweet William

TOXIC ●○●○

(*Dianthus barbatus*)

J F M A M J J A S O N D

Next Spring

60°F
60°F

3 | 9
Hardiness

1-3 weeks

12-24"

Description

Sweet William is a charming flower with clusters of pink, red, and white blooms. It's perfect for kids to plant from June through September, adding lots of color to the garden in late summer. Sweet William has a sweet scent, making it a favorite for both gardeners and pollinators like bees. Its flowers look like little ruffled balls and are great for picking and arranging in small bouquets!

To Find Out More

Sweet William has been loved in gardens for centuries and is often associated with romance and friendship. Some say its name comes from a medieval knight, while others think it's named after the poet William Shakespeare. These flowers are biennials, meaning they grow one year and bloom the next. Their resilience and charming colors make sweet William a long-lasting garden favorite.

Challenge

Create a "Scent Journal"! Plant sweet William in your garden, then track how its fragrance changes throughout the day. Does it smell stronger in the morning or evening? Write down your observations in a journal. You can even compare its scent to other flowers in your garden. Try using sweet William in small bouquets to bring its lovely scent indoors, too!

Safety Note: Sweet William is beautiful, but it's not for eating! After planting or touching the flowers, give your hands a quick wash to stay safe. If you're with younger children, remind them not to taste the leaves or flowers either.

Wallflower

OXIC

Erysimum cheiri)

J F m a m J J a s o n D

55°F

6 | 9
Hardiness

1-2 weeks

12-18"

Description

Wallflowers are vibrant flowers that grow well even in poor soil, which makes them hardy and easy to care for. They come in warm shades of orange, yellow, and purple, perfect for brightening up any garden spot from June through September. Wallflowers enjoy sunny spots and can tolerate cool weather, often blooming early in spring and lasting well into summer. Their clusters of flowers look great along borders and walls!

To Find Out More

Wallflowers get their name because they often grow along walls or rocky areas where other plants struggle. In history, wallflowers were symbols of patience and resilience, as they would "wait" on the edges of gardens. Their sweet scent attracts bees, making them a pollinator-friendly choice. Interestingly, wallflowers are members of the mustard family and share some of the same traits as edible plants like broccoli and kale!

Challenge

Try a "Wallflower Experiment"! Plant your wallflowers along a garden border or wall and compare their growth with those in open soil. Keep track of their height, color, and blooming period in a journal. You can also try planting them in rocky or poorer soil to see how they adapt. Which conditions do your wallflowers like best?

Safety Note: Wallflowers are great for gardens but not for snacks! After touching them, remember to wash your hands well. If you're gardening with younger kids, help them stay safe by reminding them not to eat any part of the plant.

Cyclamen
(Cyclamen hederifolium)

TOXIC

≥50°F
≤60°F
≥50°F
≤60°F

5 **9**
Hardiness

1–3 months

4–8"

Description
Cyclamen is a beautiful plant with delicate flowers in shades of pink, red, and white that bloom in the fall or winter. Its heart-shaped leaves are dark green with unique patterns. Cyclamen loves cooler weather and shady spots, making it perfect for growing indoors or in gardens. These flowers grow from tubers and need special care with watering during dormancy, but they bloom beautifully with the right attention!

To Find Out More
Cyclamen hederifolium is native to the Mediterranean region, including Italy, Greece, and parts of Turkey, where it grows in cool, shady forests. The plant has a fascinating growth cycle—it goes dormant in the hot summer months, storing energy in its underground tuber, then blooms again in cooler weather. *Cyclamen hederifolium* has been grown for centuries as a decorative plant, but did you know that its tubers and roots are toxic to pets and humans? Despite this, it remains a favorite for indoor gardening because of its long-lasting blooms.

Challenge
Start a *Cyclamen hederifolium* care project! Track its growth through the seasons and note when it goes dormant. Experiment carefully with watering schedules to see how the plant reacts to different amounts of water during its active growth and dormancy periods. Keep a *Cyclamen hederifolium* care journal and share your findings with friends!

Safety Note: *Cyclamen's* roots, called tubers, can be dangerous if someone eats them. When you're helping this plant grow, be sure to wear gloves and wash your hands afterward. Also, make sure pets or younger kids don't dig around where it's planted!

Decorative Cabbage
(Brassica oleracea)

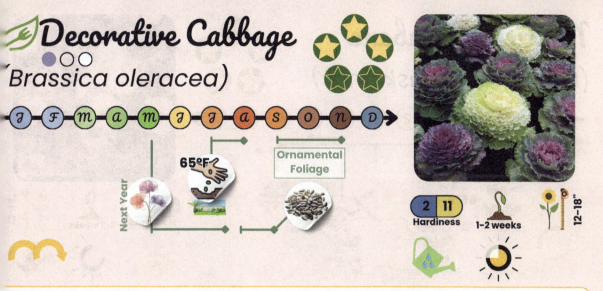

J F M A M J J A S O N D

Next Year

65°F

Ornamental Foliage

2 | 11
Hardiness

1-2 weeks

12-18"

Description
Decorative cabbages are colorful plants with big, leafy "flowers" that look a bit like giant roses! They're fun for kids to plant from June through September, adding an unusual touch to the garden. Decorative cabbages come in shades of purple, white, and green and can handle cool weather, which makes them a favorite for fall. They're perfect for kids who want a unique, colorful addition to their garden!

To Find Out More
Decorative cabbages are part of the same family as edible cabbage, broccoli, and kale, but they're grown for their looks, not their taste! Their colors often become more vibrant in cooler weather, making them ideal for late-summer or fall gardens. These "flowering" cabbages can last through mild frosts, bringing color to the garden even as other plants start to fade. They're a great example of how even vegetables can be decorative!

Challenge
Create a "Cool Weather Garden"! Plant decorative cabbages alongside other cool-weather plants and watch how their colors change as temperatures drop. Try placing them in sunny and shady spots to see which brings out the most vibrant colors. Want to take it further? If you live in a mild winter area (Hardiness Zone 7 or above), try leaving some cabbages to overwinter and grow tall stems for flowers next spring. You can even collect seeds in late summer!

Mexican Fleabane
(Erigeron karvinskianus)

J F m a m J J a s o n D

65°F

Blooming... | ... Same Year | ... Next Year

6 9 Hardiness 2-3 weeks 12-18"

Description
Mexican fleabane, or *Erigeron karvinskianus*, is a cheerful little flower that changes color as it blooms! Starting out white, it turns pink and then light purple. This plant doesn't need too much care and grows best in sunny or partly shaded spots. It's perfect for small gardens and attracts helpful bees and butterflies. Mexican fleabane grows about 12-18 inches tall and flowers from spring to fall, bringing color to your garden for months!

To Find Out More
Mexican fleabane is full of secrets, starting with its curious name! "Fleabane" comes from an old belief that this plant could repel fleas. Originating from the sunny regions of Mexico and Central America, it has a knack for attracting pollinators like bees and butterflies. And its colors? The petals shift from white to pink to purple as they open, almost like a secret code in bloom. Can you find out why it changes colors? The answer might surprise you!

Challenge
Try planting Mexican fleabane in two spots—one in full sun and the other in partial shade. Watch and record how the colors change and the flowers grow in each location. Once the flowers bloom, press the colorful petals to make a nature-inspired bookmark! You can also harvest some seeds to sow next spring and observe how they do. Will they grow differently in the new season?

Forget-me-not
Myosotis sylvatica)

J F m a m J J a s o n D

Next Year

3 8
Hardiness

1-2 weeks

6-12"

Description
Forget-me-nots are small, blue flowers that bloom in clusters during the spring. They love shady spots and moist soil, making them perfect for woodland gardens or shady flower beds. These flowers are easy to grow and spread quickly, creating a beautiful carpet of blue. Forget-me-nots are known for their cute name, their long-lasting blooms, and their preference for cooler temperatures during germination (ideally between 60-65°F).

To Find Out More
Myosotis, or forget-me-not, has been a symbol of love and remembrance for centuries. The flowers are named after a German legend in which a knight, while picking the flowers for his love, fell into a river and asked her to "forget him not" before being swept away. Forget-me-nots are often planted in memory gardens. They grow in cool, shady areas and attract pollinators like bees in the early spring. Plus, the petals are edible and can be used to decorate cakes and salads!

Challenge
Create a memory garden with forget-me-nots! Plant them in shady spots and see how quickly they spread. You can also experiment with using the petals as a garnish for desserts or salads. Keep a garden journal to track the flowers' growth and note which pollinators visit them in early spring.

California Poppy
(Eschscholzia californica)

TOXIC

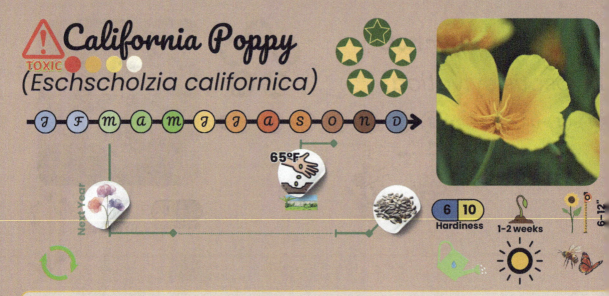

J F m a m J J a S O n D

65°F

Next Year

6 | 10
Hardiness

1-2 weeks

6-12"

Description

California poppies are bright, cheerful flowers with orange, yellow, or red petals. They bloom in the spring and summer and love sunny, dry spots. California poppies close their petals at night and open them again in the morning. These flowers are easy to grow and add a burst of color to your garden!

To Find Out More

Eschscholzia californica, or California poppy, is the state flower of California and is known for its ability to thrive in dry, sunny environments. The flowers have a unique behavior—they close up in the evening and on cloudy days, a process known as nyctinasty. Native Americans used California poppies for medicinal purposes, making teas to help with sleep and pain. These plants are also drought-tolerant, making them perfect for low-water gardens!

Challenge

Create a low-water garden with California poppies! Plant them in sunny spots and observe how the flowers close and open depending on the weather. Track their growth and experiment with watering schedules to see how little water they need. Keep a photo diary of the flowers opening each morning!

Safety Note: California poppies are super cheerful, but don't nibble on them! After spending time planting or watering, give your hands a good wash. If younger siblings or friends are helping, make sure they know to keep the flowers out of their mouths.

Peony Poppy

TOXIC ● ● ● ○

Papaver paeoniflorum)

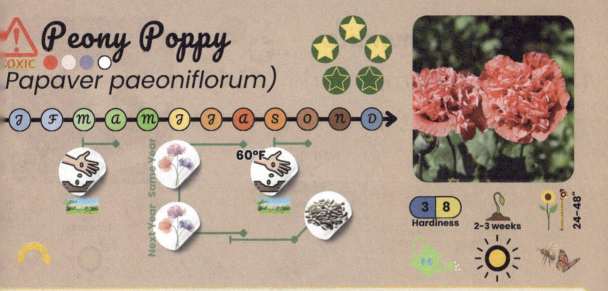

J F m a m J J a s o n D

Next Year Same Year

60°F

3 | 8
Hardiness

2-3 weeks

24-48"

Description

Peony poppies are large, beautiful flowers with distinctive ruffled petals that resemble both a peony and a poppy! Sow them in spring or fall to add soft colors like pink, red, and white to the garden in summer. These flowers grow well in sunny spots and well-drained soil, creating a stunning display. Plus, peony poppies are known for attracting bees and butterflies, making the garden even more lively! However, the plant can be toxic to pets and humans, so handle it with care.

To Find Out More

Did you know peony poppies have a long history of use in traditional gardens? Their scientific name, *Papaver paeoniflorum*, reflects their resemblance to the peony. These flowers are annuals, but they reseed easily, so they can return each year without replanting! Their big blooms make them a favorite for pollinators, and their seed heads add interest to the garden even after the flowers fade.

Challenge

Try a "Seed Head Experiment"! After your peony poppies bloom, let a few flowers turn into seed heads. Collect some seeds to plant in a new part of the garden or give to a friend. Keep track of where you planted your first peony poppies and see if they return next season. This way, you can enjoy peony poppies year after year, even though they're annuals!

Safety Note: Peony poppies have pretty flowers, but their seeds and parts can be harmful if eaten. Be sure to wash your hands after working with them, and help younger kids remember not to play with or eat the seeds.

Wild Chamomile
(Matricaria chamomilla)

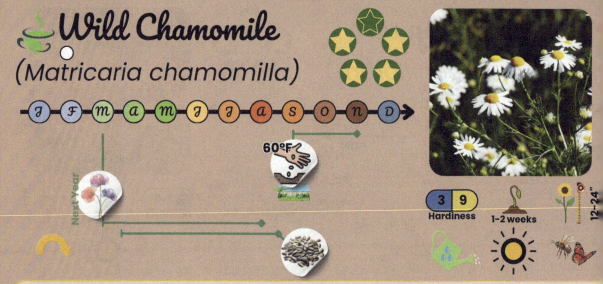

J F **m** **a** **m** **J** **J** **a** **S** **O** **n** D

60°F

Next Year

3 9 Hardiness · 1-2 weeks · 12-24"

Description

Wild chamomile is a cheerful plant with tiny, daisy-like flowers that smell like fresh apples! Sow it from March to April indoors or June to August outdoors, and you'll see blooms 6-8 weeks after sprouting. Wild chamomile grows easily in sunny spots, even in poor soil, and its flowers attract pollinators, making it a friendly addition to any garden. Known for its calming properties, it's also used in herbal teas, but remember—everything's best in moderation!

To Find Out More

Wild chamomile has been valued for centuries as a gentle herb. In ancient times, it was used to calm the stomach and help people relax. Its Latin name, *Matricaria chamomilla*, means "mother herb" because it's so soothing. Wild chamomile can grow almost anywhere, even in cracks in the pavement! Be sure to enjoy it responsibly—a cup of tea here and there is safe, but too much can cause mild reactions.

Challenge

Create a "Chamomile Harvest"! Once your wild chamomile flowers bloom, pick a few and dry them to make a simple herbal tea. Track the process in a journal, from bloom to drying. With permission, try brewing a cup and describe the taste. This experiment lets you enjoy a calming treat straight from the garden!

Virginia Bluebell
Mertensia virginica)

J F m a m J J a s o n D →

3 8 **Hardiness**

1–3 months

12–18"

Description

Virginia bluebells are beautiful, bell-shaped flowers that start as pink buds and turn bright blue when they bloom. These plants love shady areas and bloom in early spring, adding color to the forest floor or your garden. Bluebells are easy to grow and need moist soil to stay happy. They're also great for attracting butterflies and bees!

To Find Out More

Virginia bluebells have a neat color-changing trick! When the flowers first appear, they are pink. But as they grow, they slowly turn a bright blue. This happens because of a change in the flower's pigments due to the soil's acidity. Bluebells are also "ephemeral," which means they only bloom for a short time before disappearing until next spring. Native to North America, these flowers are favorites of early spring pollinators.

Challenge

Plant your own bluebells and try to capture their color-changing magic! Take photos every day from the time the buds appear to when they fully bloom. Create a time-lapse to show how the pink buds turn blue. You can even compare how fast they change color in different areas of your garden, depending on sunlight or soil type!

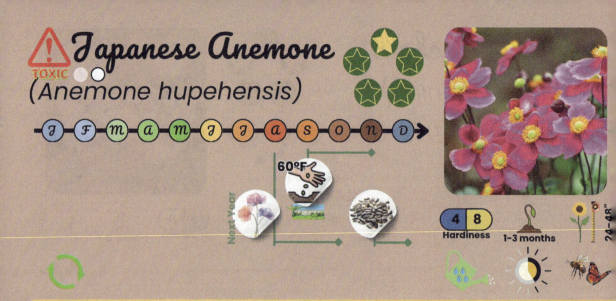

⚠ Japanese Anemone
TOXIC ⚫⚪
(Anemone hupehensis)

J F M A M J J A S O N D →

60°F

Next Year

4 | 8
Hardiness

1–3 months

24–48"

Description

Japanese anemones are tall, elegant flowers that bloom in shades of pink and white. They bloom in late summer and fall, adding color to your garden when most other flowers are done for the season. Japanese anemones love partial shade and moist soil, making them perfect for woodland gardens.

To Find Out More

Anemone hupehensis, or Japanese anemone, is native to China and Japan and is known for its delicate, graceful flowers. These plants bloom in the fall, providing much-needed color in shady gardens. Japanese anemones are also great for attracting late-season pollinators like bees and butterflies. The name anemone comes from the Greek word for "wind," as the flowers often sway in the breeze. However, the plant can be toxic to pets and humans, so handle it with care.

Challenge

Design a woodland garden with Japanese anemones! Plant them in a shaded spot and track their growth. Observe which pollinators visit in the fall, and experiment with different levels of shade and moisture. Record your findings in a garden journal!

Safety Note: Japanese anemones can cause vomiting and diarrhea if ingested. Even touching the plant's sap can irritate the skin. Always wear gloves when handling any part of the plant, including leaves, stems, and seeds. Avoid licking or putting fingers near your mouth after touching the plant, and remember to wash your hands thoroughly afterward. This is a great reminder to be cautious around certain plants!

Chapter 6

Year-Round Garden Care

Chapter 6 focuses on maintaining a thriving butterfly garden year-round, addressing seasonal care, pest and disease management, eco-friendly solutions, and creating a butterfly-friendly sanctuary. It emphasizes natural remedies, sustainable practices, and proactive preparation for winter and spring, guiding readers to nurture vibrant, resilient plants while supporting pollinators.

Year-Round Butterfly Garden Care

Seasonal Care for a Thriving Garden

Gardening is a year-round adventure! Each season brings unique tasks to keep your flowers healthy and your butterfly garden buzzing with life. Here's how to care for your garden through the seasons:

- **Winter:** In colder regions, protect young plants with frost covers. Hardy flowers like hellebores can still bloom. Use this time to plan for spring!

- **Spring:** Time to wake up your garden! Sow seeds like sunflowers and marigolds, remove weeds before they spread, and enrich the soil with compost.

- **Summer:** Long sunny days mean your flowers need extra water. Water deeply, deadhead faded blooms, and keep an eye out for pests. Companion planting can help manage bugs naturally.

- **Autumn:** Prep for colder months by planting late bloomers like asters. Collect seeds for next year and mulch beds to protect roots from frost.

> **Tip:** Keep a journal to track seasonal changes in your garden and make notes on what works best for each season!

A Mourning Cloak butterfly can live up to 12 months.

Did you know? Certain species of butterflies like the **Mourning Cloak (Nymphalis antiopa)** can hibernate during winter, hiding in hollow plant stems or under loose tree bark!

Challenge: Can you research and find out which butterfly species in your area hibernate, especially those endangered? Then, explore the plant list in this book or look around your garden to identify which plants could help these butterflies thrive. What could you add to make your garden even more butterfly-friendly?

Caring for Your Garden All Year Long

> **Tip:** Mix plants with different seasonal needs in the same space to ensure blooms year-round and make maintenance a breeze!

As spring begins, sow seeds indoors for an early start, and prepare your soil to give flowers a strong foundation.

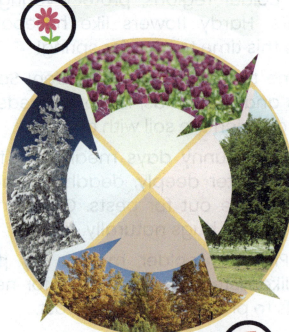

Shield fragile plants with frost covers or mulch to protect roots from freezing.

Water deeply in the morning o[r] evening to keep plants hydrate[d] and preven[t] evaporation.

Collect seeds from mature plants for next season, and add late bloomers like asters to your garden before the frost.

Did you know? Some flowers, like asters and marigolds, are double-duty champions—they bloom late into the season and provide vital nectar for migrating butterflies!

With your garden thriving across the seasons, it's important to watch for challenges. Let's explore ways to identify and manage pests and diseases naturally, while keeping your garden safe for pollinators!

Curious about how to help endangered butterflies? Keep reading to discover fun ways to make your garden a haven for them!

Keep Your Garden Healthy, Naturally

Gardens are full of life, but pests and diseases can be uninvited guests. With natural methods, you can keep your garden thriving while protecting pollinators like butterflies.

Common Pests and Solutions

- **Aphids (Spring to Early Summer):** These tiny green, black, or white insects suck sap from plants, causing leaves to curl and yellow. They are especially active in mild weather.

A colony of aphids.

  - **Solution:** Attract ladybugs, which feast on aphids, or spray plants with a mix of water and a few drops of dish soap.

- **Caterpillars (Mid to Late Spring):** Butterfly caterpillars are welcome guests—they feed on host plants like milkweed to grow into beautiful butterflies. However, some caterpillars, such as **cabbage worms**, can damage other plants.

A cabbage worm.

  - **Solution:** Handpick harmful caterpillars like cabbage worms (green and active on leafy vegetables) and relocate them to an area where they won't harm your garden. Use row covers to protect vulnerable plants.
  - **Encourage Good Caterpillars!** For butterfly species, provide host plants and remember their munching is part of the garden's ecosystem.

- **Slugs and Snails (Spring to Early Autumn):** These pests thrive in cool, moist conditions, chewing holes in leaves and stems. They are most active at night or after rain.
  - **Solution:** Sprinkle sand, fine gravel, or crushed eggshells or coffee grounds around plants to deter them. Water in the morning to avoid creating damp conditions at night.

These nice snail and slug can get very hungry on your plants!

Did you know? Snails have thousands of tiny teeth and use them to eat through leaves!

Think About It: Explore which butterflies live in your area and need your help! Search online to identify their caterpillars and learn about the plants they like. Then, create a butterfly-friendly space in your garden to support them at every stage of their life cycle!

Common Diseases and Remedies

In late spring, watch out for powdery mildew on tightly spaced plants. Summer's heat can exacerbate root rot in overwatered soil.

> **Tip:** Keep an eye out for early signs of disease like spots, yellowing, or wilting. Acting quickly can save your plants and keep your garden thriving!

- **Powdery Mildew (Late Spring to Summer):** This white fungus often appears on leaves in humid conditions.
  - **Solution:** Improve airflow by spacing plants and water only at the base of plants. Alternately, use a homemade solution of baking soda and water as a natural treatment.

Leaves coated with white fungal spots

- **Black Spot (Spring to Autumn):** Dark fungal spots often appear on rose leaves.
  - **Solution:** Prune affected leaves and spray neem oil to prevent spread. Remove and dispose of infected leaves carefully to avoid spreading the fungus. Never add affected leaves to your compost!

Dark fungal spots on rose leaves.

- **Root Rot (Anytime):** This fungal issue can occur anytime soil remains waterlogged, especially during the rainy season or with overwatering in summer. It causes plants to wilt.
  - **Solution:** Ensure soil drains well and avoid overwatering. Consider sand to improve drainage.

Wilting caused by rotting roots due to overwatering.

Did you know? Powdery mildew thrives in both high humidity and dry conditions, making it a common garden challenge. Proper airflow and spacing are your best defenses!

> **Fun Fact:** Some plants, like succulents, are almost immune to root rot because they store water in their leaves instead of their roots. If you're gardening in a wet climate, consider adding succulents to your garden for easy care!

Challenge: Explore which diseases are most common in your region and may affect your garden! What steps can you take to protect your garden from them? Write down possible solutions, and later on, conclude on what worked well and what you could improve!

Share your findings with friends or family and see if they've faced similar challenges in their gardens!

Eco-Friendly Tips for Thriving Plants

Natural methods not only protect your garden but also support local ecosystems and keep harmful chemicals out of the environment. Nature provides everything you need for thriving flowers and butterflies—let us explore some simple techniques!

Top Natural Gardening Methods

1. Homemade Insect Sprays:
- **Dish Soap Spray:** Mix water and soap for aphids.
- **Garlic Spray:** Blend garlic with water, strain, and spray to repel pests, because garlic's strong smell masks the scent of plants, confusing pests.

2. Companion Planting: Grow plants that help each other.
- **Examples:** Marigolds repel nematodes, which are tiny worms that can damage plant roots by feeding on them, weakening your plants over time. Meanwhile, borage attracts pollinators.
- **Benefit:** This technique also encourages biodiversity, making your garden more resilient.

3. Mulching: Protect soil, retain moisture, and reduce weeds.
- Use straw, wood chips, or grass clippings to create an effective mulch layer. Try collecting fallen leaves in autumn to create your own mulch!

4. Composting: Turn kitchen scraps into rich compost to feed your plants.
- Turn food and yard waste into compost by keeping it moist and aerated. Within months, you'll have nutrient-rich soil.

5. Row Covers: Use mesh or netting to protect plants while letting sunlight in.
- **Benefit:** Row covers keep pests out while protecting plants from sudden weather changes.

Did you know? Composting reduces waste and enriches soil. Start your compost pile with fruit peels, eggshells, and yard clippings! Compost can get warm enough to steam on cold mornings—It's like a cozy blanket for your soil—keeping it warm and full of nutrients!

Think About It: Can you create a homemade pest spray using ingredients from your kitchen, like garlic or soap? Try it on a small part of your garden and track its effects. Did it work? Which pests stayed away, and what would you do differently next time?

Create a Butterfly Sanctuary

Butterflies need more than just flowers—they need food, water, and shelter to thrive. Learn how to make your garden a butterfly's favorite home!

Essentials for Butterflies

1. Food:
- Include nectar-rich flowers like **zinnias**, **cosmos**, and **alyssum** to provide butterflies with year-round nourishment.
- **Milkweed** is an essential host plant for monarch butterflies, *even though it's not among the 36 flowers highlighted in this book.*

2. Water:
- Make a "butterfly puddling station" with a shallow dish of wet sand.
- Butterflies are drawn to lightly salted water puddles too! Adding a pinch of salt to the water makes it more attractive.

3. Shelter:
- Provide shrubs, tall grasses, or rock piles for resting spots.
- In winter, leave some dried stems or leaf piles for butterflies to hide in.
- Install butterfly houses for extra protection.

 Caution: Avoid chemical pesticides—they can harm butterflies and other pollinators!

A Monarch feeding on Swamp Milkweed.

Fun Fact: Milkweed not only feed monarch butterflies and thei caterpillars but also produces fluff seeds when its pods open—perfec for observing nature's cycles up close!

Tip: Place butterfly-friendly plants in sunny spots, where they can bask and warm up for flight!

Challenge: Observe your garden and list which butterfly species visit. Use a notebook to record what you see! What can you add to make them stay longer or support their life cycle?

Get Your Garden Ready for the Seasons

Winter offers a quiet moment to ready your garden for a vibrant spring. A little effort now brings big rewards later!

Winter Preparation

1. Tidy Up:

- Remove dead plants and fallen leaves to reduce pests.
- Leave seed heads and stems for wildlife.

2. Mulch:

- Add a layer of mulch to insulate roots and enrich soil.
- Helps retain soil moisture during winter frosts.

Spring Planning

1. Seed Indoors:

- Start primrose, trailing lobelia and aster seeds indoors for early blooms.
- Once the danger of frost has passed, move your indoor seedlings outdoors for a colorful spring garden! Learn more about this in **Chapter 5 — Plant Selection Guide**.

2. Soil Testing:

- Test your soil to ensure it's ready for planting. For fun experiments like "**How Can You Test for Nutrients**" or "**Check Your Soil's pH: A Simple Experiment,**" head to the "**To Go Further**" section in **Chapter 2 — The Life Cycle of a Plant**!

Lovely pink primroses in snow.

Did you know? Many butterflies start their lifecycle early in the year. Having flowers ready in spring helps them thrive! Planning ahead means your garden will be ready just in time to welcome these pollinators back!

Think About It: What flowers can you start indoors during winter to give your spring garden a head start? Think about which flowers might bloom early and support pollinators like butterflies.

Chapter 7

Fun Activities in the Garden

Chapter 7 encourages young gardeners to deepen their connection with nature through hands-on activities. It includes keeping a gardening journal, crafting with garden materials, exploring insects, and building an insect hotel. Fun recipes and seed-saving tips inspire creativity, while raising caterpillars and observing butterflies teach the wonders of metamorphosis and pollination. Young gardeners will uncover secrets of the garden while contributing to its thriving ecosystem!

Create Your Gardening Journal

Record Your Garden Adventures!

A gardening journal is a scrapbook to track plants, growth, and visiting creatures. Your gardening journal will grow alongside your garden, becoming a treasured keepsake!

What You'll Need

- A notebook or binder.
- Markers, crayons, or colored pencils.
- Stickers or pressed flowers for decoration.
- Photos of your garden or yourself in your garden.
- Graph paper or printed charts to track plant growth.

Step-by-Step Instructions

1. Choose Your Journal: Pick a notebook or binder that you can decorate and customize.

2. Decorate the Cover: Use drawings, stickers, or pressed flowers to make it uniquely yours. Add your name and the year.

3. Create Sections: Inside your journal, divide it into sections for:

- Flower names and planting dates indoors and outdoors.
- Weather observations.
- Daily and weekly garden notes.
- Sketches or growth charts for your plants.
- Butterfly or insect sightings.

4. Note critical information: Last frost date, your hardiness zone.

5. Add Observations: Note what works and what doesn't. Did a flower bloom earlier than expected?

6. Get Creative: Use colorful markers, stickers, or pressed leaves to make each page lively and exciting.

Find ready-made garden journal templates online or on Amazon!

Did you know? Garden journaling helps you plan better gardens. It's like a time capsule for your gardening skills!

Seasonal Nature Crafts

Celebrate Your Garden!

Nature crafts bring your garden indoors with seasonal materials. Explore the changing seasons and create something special to enjoy or gift!

What You'll Need

- Flowers like pansies or marigolds (fresh or dried).
- Pinecones and colorful autumn leaves.
- Dried lavender or chamomile for sachets.
- Sturdy wire for wreaths.
- Cardstock or bookmarks for pressed flowers.
- Glue, scissors, and craft paper.

Step-by-Step Instructions

Winter - Sachets

- Dry lavender or chamomile flowers.
- Fill small fabric bags with the dried flowers.
- Tie the bag tightly, and use it as a scented sachet for drawers or as a gift.

Spring - Pressed Flower Bookmarks

- Pick small fresh flowers like violas or alyssums.
- Place them between sheets of paper and press them in a heavy book for a week.
- Once dried, glue them onto a strip of cardstock.

Summer - Floral Wreaths

- Gather fresh flowers like sunflowers, zinnias, or marigolds.
- Shape a sturdy wire into a circular base.
- Attach the flowers using floral tape or string. Hang your wreath for cheerful summer vibes.

Autumn - Leaf Centerpieces

- Collect colorful leaves, pinecones, and acorns.
- Arrange them in a shallow bowl with candles in the center for a festive touch.

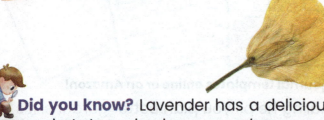

Did you know? Lavender has a delicious scent and is often used in sachets to make drawers and spaces smell fresh and pleasant!

Exploring Garden Inhabitants

Discover the Creatures in Your Garden!

Your garden hosts fascinating creatures. If you observe them, you will learn how they help keep your garden healthy while revealing the amazing balance of nature.

What You'll Need

- A magnifying glass.
- A small notebook or journal.
- Colored pencils or crayons for sketching.
- A guidebook or app to identify insects and other creatures.
- A shallow dish for observing soil critters (optional).

Step-by-Step Instructions

1. Observe Pollinators: Watch bees and butterflies gather nectar. Notice how they move between flowers and collect pollen.

2. Examine Garden Helpers: Use a magnifying glass to study earthworms or ladybugs. How do they help plants?

3. Record Your Findings: Draw or describe each creature in your journal. Note the time, location, and flowers they prefer.

4. Investigate Soil Life: Carefully dig a small area to find ants or tiny critters. Gently return them to their home afterward.

5. Research Together: Use a guidebook or app to learn about the creatures you observed. What role do they play in your garden?

Discovering garden helpers up close!

Did you know? Ladybugs eat up to 50 aphids a day, making them your garden's natural pest control heroes!

Tip: Create a "Creature Tracker" in your journal to log the insects, birds, and small animals you find. Include dates and any unique observations.

Making an Insect Hotel

Create a Cozy Home for Helpful Insects!

Insects like bees and ladybugs are essential garden helpers—they control pests, pollinate flowers, and keep your garden thriving.

What You'll Need

- A small wooden box or an old shoe box.
- Hollow bamboo sticks, pinecones, or straw.
- Small twigs or bark pieces.
- Dry leaves, moss, or hay.
- Wire mesh (optional, to keep materials secure).
- Scissors, glue, or a stapler.

Step-by-Step Instructions

1. Choose Your Base: Use a sturdy box or carton as your hotel frame. Ensure it's waterproof or placed in a sheltered spot.

2.Fill It Up: Tightly arrange bamboo sticks, pinecones, twigs, and straw inside the box to create small spaces for insects to hide.

3. Add Cozy Touches: Create layers of dry leaves, moss, or hay to make the hotel more inviting for tiny creatures.

4. Secure Materials: Use glue or wire mesh to hold everything in place so it doesn't fall out.

5. Find the Perfect Spot: Place your insect hotel in a sunny spot near flowers or plants to attract helpful garden visitors.

Example of a beautifully designed insect hotel ready to welcome helpful insects.

Did you know? Bees and ladybugs use insect hotels to rest, lay eggs, or hibernate. Ladybugs also eat harmful pests like aphids, protecting your plants.

Tip: Get creative! Paint your insect hotel with bright, non-toxic colors to make it a cheerful and inviting addition to your garden.

Recipes and Use of Garden Plants

Turn Your Harvest into Tasty Treats!

Your garden is full of edible treasures! Transform flowers and plants into creative recipes for snacks, drinks, or decorations.

What You'll Need

- **For Nasturtium Salad:** Nasturtium flowers and leaves, salad greens, olive oil, lemon juice, and salt for dressing.
- **For Borage Lemonade:** Fresh borage flowers, lemons, sugar or honey, water, ice cubes

Step-by-Step Instructions

1. Prepare Nasturtium Salad

- Wash nasturtium flowers and leaves thoroughly.
- Mix them with your favorite salad greens.
- Drizzle olive oil, lemon juice, and a pinch of salt for a colorful, peppery-flavored salad.

2. Make Borage Lemonade

- Wash fresh borage flowers and set aside a few for garnish.
- Squeeze the juice of 2-3 lemons into a pitcher.
- Add sugar or honey to taste and stir until dissolved.
- Fill the pitcher with cold water and ice cubes. Add the borage flowers for a light cucumber-like flavor and a beautiful garnish.

A tasty nasturtium salad.

Challenge: Can you prepare your very own cup of chamomile tea?
- Pick fresh chamomile flowers and rinse them gently.
- Steep a handful in hot water for 5-7 minutes.
- Pour your tea and enjoy!

Record your process and flavor notes in your gardening journal. Did you like it? Try adding honey or lemon for a twist!

> **Tip:** You can dry chamomile flowers to make tea anytime! Spread them on a clean cloth, let them dry in a sunny spot and store them in an airtight container.

Raising Caterpillars

Experience the Magic of Metamorphosis!

Watching caterpillars grow into butterflies is magical. By raising them, you'll discover their lifecycle while helping pollinators thrive. It's an exciting way to connect with nature!

What You'll Need

- Milkweed or specific host plants for caterpillars.
- A clear container with air holes (like a jar or terrarium).
- Fresh leaves from the host plant for feeding.
- A soft paintbrush for handling caterpillars (optional).
- A journal for observations.

Step-by-Step Instructions

1. Find Caterpillars: Search for caterpillars on host plants like milkweed (for monarchs). Gently pick one or two to raise.

2. Prepare Their Home: Place the caterpillars in a clear container with air holes. Add fresh leaves from their host plant for food.

3. Feed Them Daily: Replace the leaves daily with fresh ones. Make sure to remove uneaten leaves to keep the container clean.

4. Observe the Changes: Watch as the caterpillars grow, molt, and form a chrysalis. Record your observations in your journal!

5. Release the Butterfly: Once the butterfly emerges, let its wings dry for a few hours before releasing it into your garden.

The life cycle of a Monarch: Caterpillar stage, chrysalis, butterfly (from left to right).

Tip: Place your container near indirect sunlight, but avoid direct heat to keep the caterpillars comfortable.

Did you know? A caterpillar grows up to 100 times its original size before becoming a butterfly!

Collect Seeds to Replant Them Next Year

Save Summer's Magic for Next Spring!

Collecting seeds from your garden is like saving a piece of summer to enjoy again. This simple activity teaches you how to gather, dry, and store seeds so you can replant them next year and watch your garden grow anew!

What You'll Need

- Paper envelopes or small jars for storing seeds.
- Scissors or garden clippers.
- A dry cloth or paper towel for drying seeds.
- A marker for labeling envelopes or jars.
- A notebook to record seed collection dates.

Step-by-Step Instructions

1. Choose Your Flowers: Select flowers like sunflowers, marigolds, or zinnias. Look for blooms with dry, faded petals and seed heads that are beginning to dry out.

2. Harvest the Seeds: Use scissors or garden clippers to cut the seed heads from the plants. Be gentle to avoid damaging the seeds.

3. Dry the Seeds: Spread the seed heads on a dry cloth or paper towel in a cool, airy spot. Let them dry completely for 1-2 weeks.

4. Extract: Gently separate the seeds from the seed heads.

5. Store: Place them in paper envelopes or jars, and label each with the flower name and date.

6. Plan for Next Year: Keep your seeds in a cool, dry place until spring. Use your gardening journal to plan where and when to plant them!

Did you know? Some seeds, like sunflowers, can also be snacks for birds. Leave a few seed heads in your garden to feed wildlife over the winter!

> **Tip:** When labeling seed envelopes, include the flower name, the collection date, and any special notes, like "best in full sun" or "easy to grow."

Saving seeds today: more flowers tomorrow!

Butterfly Detective Challenge

Spot Butterflies and Learn Their Secrets!

Butterflies bring magic to your garden with their fluttering wings and bright colors. By observing them closely, you can uncover the secrets of their behavior and even help them thrive!

What You'll Need

- A notebook or journal to record your observations.
- A magnifying glass (optional).
- A field guide or app to identify butterflies.
- A sunny spot with blooming flowers.

Step-by-Step Instructions

1. Find a Butterfly-Friendly Spot: Look for flowers like zinnias, marigolds, or milkweed in a sunny location. Butterflies love them!

2. Observe Carefully: Watch how butterflies feed on nectar and flutter between flowers. Note their colors, patterns, and wing shapes.

3. Take Notes: Write down your observations in your journal. What time of day are they most active? Which flowers do they prefer?

4. Research Their Behavior: Use a guide or app to identify the butterflies you see. Learn about their host plants and migration patterns.

5. Create a Butterfly Haven: Plant flowers they love or set up a shallow dish of water with pebbles for them to rest and sip from.

Challenge: Can you discover how many different butterflies visit your garden in 30 minutes or an hour? Pick a sunny time of day and record their colors and behaviors. Bonus: Create a checklist or draw your favorite butterfly in your journal!

Zinnias and marigolds, a butterfly treat!

Did you know? Butterflies can see colors we can't, like ultraviolet light! This helps them find flowers with the most nectar.

Tip: Plant a mix of flowers that bloom at different times, and your garden will be like an all-you-can-eat buffet for butterflies!

Conclusion

Your Gardening Adventure Continues!

Hey young gardeners! 🌱 Your garden is just the beginning of an amazing adventure. Every seed you plant, every flower you grow, and every insect you watch helps create a more beautiful, colorful world. Gardening isn't just about plants—it's about discovery, creativity, and making a difference.

Remember, with each small step, you're helping butterflies find a home, giving bees a reason to buzz, and creating a space where nature thrives. So, grab your journal, plant your seeds, and keep exploring—you're a real Earth Hero!

A Note for Parents and Educators

Gardening offers children so much more than just fresh air and fun. It nurtures their emotional growth in profound ways, aligning with the emotional profiles defined by Professor Richard Davidson: Positive Outlook, Attention, Resilience, and Sensitivity to Context. Through gardening, children cultivate patience as they wait for seeds to sprout, sharpen their focus as they observe the life cycle of a plant, and build resilience as they face challenges like weeds and pests.

These activities also foster a deep connection with nature, encouraging children to care for the environment and see themselves as stewards of the Earth. At a time when teaching sustainability and mindfulness is more important than ever, gardening offers a perfect way to inspire these values.

By gardening together, we can teach the next generation not only to grow plants but to grow themselves—stronger, more attentive, and more in tune with the world around them. This journey helps plant seeds of curiosity, creativity, and care in the hearts of young gardeners everywhere.

Glossary

Term	Definition	Page(s)
Annual	Plants that complete their life cycle in one year.	13, 15
Annual (symbol)	A plant that completes its life cycle, from germination to seed production, in a single year.	72
Annual Weeds	Weeds that complete their life cycle in one year.	53
Biennial	Plants that take two years to complete their life cycle.	13, 15, 16
Biennial (symbol)	A plant that completes its life cycle over two years, typically flowering in the second year.	72
Biennial Weeds	Weeds that take two years to complete their life cycle.	53
Black Spot	A fungal disease that creates dark spots on leaves, commonly affecting roses.	116
Bloom Time	The specific months during which a plant flowers and displays its colors.	71
Borage Lemonade	A refreshing drink made with borage flowers, lemons, sugar or honey, and ice.	127

Term	Definition	Page(s)
Broadcast Sowing	A method of sowing seeds by scattering them evenly across soil surface for natural growth patterns.	44
Butterfly Puddling Station	A shallow dish with wet sand or water for butterflies to drink and gather nutrients.	118
Butterfly-Friendly Spot	A garden area designed to attract and support butterflies with nectar-rich flowers.	130
Caterpillar Raising	The process of nurturing caterpillars into butterflies to learn about their lifecycle.	128
Clover	Fixes nitrogen in the soil and provides nectar for pollinators.	55
Cold Stratification	A process where seeds are exposed to cold conditions to simulate winter, helping them germinate when conditions warm.	71
Companion Planting	The practice of growing certain plants together to benefit each other.	117
Compost	Organic matter like decomposed plants or food scraps used to enrich soil nutrients.	42
Composting	The process of decomposing organic materials into nutrient-rich soil.	34
Cross-Pollination	Pollen exchange between flowers for genetic diversity.	20

Term	Definition	Page(s)
Deadhead	The process of removing faded or dead flowers to encourage new growth.	114
Drought-Tolerant (symbol)	A plant's ability to survive with minimal water once established.	72
Edibility	The quality of a plant being safe to eat, often noted in flowers or leaves used for culinary purposes.	74
Friendly Neighbor Flowers	Plants that grow well together, helping each other by sharing resources or attracting beneficial insects.	67
Full Sun (symbol)	A light condition where plants receive 6 or more hours of sunlight daily.	72
Gardening Journal	A personal record to track gardening activities, growth, and observations.	123
Germinate	The process of a seed starting to grow.	23
Hardiness Zone	A geographic area defined by the lowest average temperatures, used to determine which plants can thrive in that region.	60
Herbal Tea (symbol)	A beverage made from the infusion of plant leaves, flowers, or seeds, often with medicinal properties.	74
Individual Planting	Planting larger seeds like sunflowers individually at the recommended depth for strong growth.	45

Term	Definition	Page(s)
Indoor Planting	Planting seeds indoors in trays or pots before transplanting them outside once conditions improve.	39
Insect Hotel	A shelter created to provide habitat for helpful garden insects like ladybugs and bees.	126
Loamy Soil	A balanced mix of sand, silt, and clay, ideal for most plants.	28
Milkweed	Essential for monarch butterflies, offering nectar-rich flowers.	55
Mulch	Material like bark or leaves spread over soil to retain moisture, protect roots, regulate temperature, and suppress weeds.	42, 114
Mulching	A technique to block sunlight and prevent weed growth using organic material —Refer to Mulch	55
Nitrogen Cycle	The process of nitrogen moving through soil, plants, and air.	29
Nitrogen-Fixing Bacteria	Microbes that convert nitrogen from the air into usable forms for plants.	29
Partial Shade (symbol)	A type of light condition where plants receive 3–5 hours of sunlight daily.	72
Perennial	Plants that live for multiple years, blooming seasonally.	13, 14

Term	Definition	Page(s)
Perennial (symbol)	A plant that lives for more than two years, flowering annually after establishment.	72
Perennial Weeds	Weeds that return every year with deep roots.	53
Petals	Colorful parts of a flower that attract pollinators.	10
pH	A scale measuring the acidity or alkalinity of soil.	36
Photosynthesis	The process by which plants make food using sunlight.	24
Pistil	The central part of a flower where seeds form.	10
Plantain	Improves soil health and offers food for caterpillars.	55
Plumule	A tiny shoot pushing upward toward the light.	23
Pollination	The process by which pollen is transferred to fertilize plants.	11, 16, 20
Pollinator	An animal, like a bee or butterfly, that transfers pollen between flowers.	24, 73, 125
Powdery Mildew	A fungal disease causing white, powdery spots on plant leaves.	116
Radicle	A small root growing downward to anchor the plant.	23

Term	Definition	Page(s)
Raised Beds	Raised gardening structures that improve drainage, warmth, and control over soil quality.	43
Row Covers	Mesh or fabric used to protect plants from pests and sudden weather changes.	117
Seasonal Planning	Organizing gardening activities based on the seasons to ensure optimal growth and blooming periods.	62
Seed Collection	The act of harvesting, drying, and storing seeds for future planting.	129
Smothering	Covering the ground with materials like cardboard to block sunlight.	55
Stamens	Structures in flowers that produce pollen.	10, 13
Symbols	Icons used to represent specific plant needs, such as sunlight, water, or hardiness, to make plant care easier to understand.	70
Toxic Plants	Plants that can cause irritation, harm, or toxicity if touched or ingested, requiring caution.	48
Toxicity	A property of some plants that makes them harmful if touched or ingested. Toxic parts may include leaves, seeds, or sap.	74
Transplanting	Moving a plant from one location (such as indoors) to another (such as outdoors) to promote growth and adaptability.	71

Thank You for Being Part of This Adventure!

I'm so happy you chose *The Inspiring Gardening Book for Kids*!

If this book inspired you, a quick review takes just 2 minutes but makes a HUGE impact!

Every review helps:

■ Other parents & teachers discover the book.
■ Support the creation of more nature-inspired books.
■ Grow a community of young gardeners!

📲 Simply scan the QR Code opposite to leave your review on Amazon. Your voice matters!

Happy Gardening!

Georges Fine

Have 2 minutes? We'd love to hear from you! Share your thoughts and help us grow by taking a quick survey. Simply scan the QR code opposite!

Let's Keep in Touch!

As your gardening journey flourishes, embark with horizonlecture.com on a nurturing path where curiosity blooms and imagination soars.

Reach out to us at contact@horizonlecture.com for questions, shared stories, or a spark of inspiration. Discover a dedicated page for "The Inspiring Gardening Book for Kids" on our site.

HorizonLecture is dedicated to fostering a love of reading in children, guiding them to explore and develop their intellectual and emotional potential, curiosity, and imagination.

The website features book recommendations that emphasize virtues such as empathy and patience, with the aim of enriching the bond between parents and children through shared reading experiences.

They also express a commitment to respecting each child's individuality in their literary journey.

Made in the USA
Monee, IL
30 March 2025

14848136R00079